CHRISTUS CONSUMMATOR.

CHRISTUS CONSUMMATOR:

SOME ASPECTS OF THE WORK AND
PERSON OF CHRIST IN RELATION
TO MODERN THOUGHT.

BY

BROOKE FOSS WESTCOTT, D.D., D.C.L.,

CANON OF WESTMINSTER AND REGIUS PROFESSOR

Wipf & Stock
PUBLISHERS
Eugene, Oregon

αὕτη ἐστὶν ἡ αἰώνιος ζωὴ ἵνα γινώσκωσι σὲ τὸν μόνον ἀληθινὸν θεόν, καὶ ὃν ἀπέστειλας Ἰησοῦν Χριστόν.

St John xvii. 3.

Wipf and Stock Publishers
199 West 8th Avenue, Suite 3
Eugene, Oregon 97401

Christus Consummator
Some Aspects of the Work and Person of Christ in Relation to Modern Thought
By Westcott, B.F.
ISBN: 1-59244-512-8
Publication date 1/29/2004
Previously published by Macmillan and Co., 1886

PREFACE.

THE Sermons in the present volume, with the exception of the last, were preached in Westminster Abbey during my residence in *August* 1885 and *January* 1886. I have endeavoured in them to guide others to lines of thought which I have myself found to lead to that sure hope which we can reach *through patience and through comfort of the Scriptures.* I have added as an Appendix a Sermon preached at Cambridge, which was designed to give a practical application of this teaching.

The broad lessons of the Epistle to the Hebrews appear to me to shew how much that seems to be loss in regard to our religious circumstances proves to be gain by turning our minds from things temporal and provisional to Christ Himself. I sought therefore first to indicate these in a general outline, and then afterwards to point out a little more in detail some special aspects of the Person and Work of Christ which correspond with the wants of our own position.

The delays, the failures, the sorrows which beset the great life of humanity can be borne gladly if we are allowed even from afar to recognise the Presence of CHRISTUS CONSUMMATOR. The things of time are transfigured in the light of eternity.

The last words of the Founder of the Abbey express with pathetic force one side of the Truth. 'Weep not,' he said to the Queen sobbing by his side, 'Weep not my daughter. For I shall not die but live; and as I leave the land of the dying, I trust to see the blessings of the Lord in the land of the living.' The vision of that unchanging order is given to us even here in the Gospel. *Father...*, the Lord said of His disciples, *This is the life eternal, that they know Thee the only true God, and Him Whom Thou didst send, even Jesus Christ.*

B. F. W.

DIVINITY SCHOOL,
CAMBRIDGE.
May 24th, 1886.

CHRISTUS CONSUMMATOR.

I.

LESSONS FROM AN EPOCH OF CHANGE.

I. *The trials of a new age.*

II. *The destiny of man fulfilled by Christ through suffering.*

III. *The King Priest.*

IV. *The Universal Society.*

V. *The New Covenant.*

II.

ASPECTS OF THE INCARNATION.

I. *The Incarnation a subject for devout study.*

II. *The Incarnation and the Creation.*

III. *The Incarnation and the Fall.*

IV. *The Incarnation and Nature.*

V. *The Incarnation and Life.*

APPENDIX.

The vision of God the call of the Prophet.

CHRISTUS CONSUMMATOR. I.

LESSONS FROM AN EPOCH OF CHANGE.

I. *The trials of a new age.*

II. *The destiny of man fulfilled by Christ through suffering.*

III. *The King Priest.*

IV. *The universal Society.*

V. *The New Covenant.*

This word, Yet once more, signifieth the removing of those things that are shaken, as of things that have been made, that those things which are not shaken may remain.

HEBR. xii. 27.

THE TRIALS OF A NEW AGE.

EVERY age which is moved by the Spirit of I.
God feels keenly the searching, chastening Did. *in Ps.* lxxxviii. 8.
power of that Divine Presence. "He that is near Me," the Lord is reported to have said, "is near fire." And we cannot hope to enjoy the splendour of a fuller, purer light without enduring the pain which necessarily comes from the removal of the veils by which it was obscured. Gain through apparent loss; victory through momentary defeat; the energy of a new life through John xvi. 21 f.
pangs of travail; such has ever been the law of spiritual progress. This law has been fulfilled in every crisis of reformation; and it is illustrated for our learning in every page of the New Testament.

But in no apostolic writing is the truth unfolded with such pathetic force as in the Epistle to the Hebrews. And so it is, I think, that that mysterious "word of consolation" appeals to us Hebr. xiii. 22.
with a voice of thrilling power in our time of

I. trial, when the law of progress, the law of fruitfulness through death, seems to be hastening to a fresh fulfilment. The student of that Epistle cannot but observe that no men were ever called upon to endure greater sacrifices, to surrender more precious hopes, to bear deeper disappointments, than those to whom it was first addressed. Men who had lived in the light of the Old Testament, men who had known the joy of a noble ritual, men who had habitually drawn near to God in intelligible ways, men who had but lately welcomed Him in Whom they believed that the glory of Israel should be consummated, were most unexpectedly required to face what seemed to them to be the forfeiture of all that they held dearest. The letter of Scripture, the worship of the temple, the expectations of national triumph, had to be abandoned. The heirs of the patriarchs, when they first felt that they were entering on their inheritance, were compelled, if they remained Christians, to accept the position of outcasts from the ancient commonwealth of God, and to confess themselves followers of One crucified and rejected, Who delayed to assume His throne.

And what then? They could not but begin to reckon up their loss and gain. The fresh
Hebr. x. 32 ff. enthusiasm of their early faith had died away in

the weary waiting of a lifetime. They had in I.
part degenerated because they had not grown. Hebr. vi. 11.
But they were not uncared for in the crisis of their peril. Out of the darkness of the gathering storm, in which the Holy Place was to be for ever swept away, came a voice which interpreted the sad riddles of their fate. Under the guidance of a nameless apostle, the Hebrews were enabled to see how the sufferings of Christ were not a difficulty in the way of His Messiahship, to be compensated by a visible triumph, but the very pledge of the fulfilment of the destiny of man in spite of sin; to see how the unbelief of Israel opened the way for the larger unfolding of the world-wide counsels of God; to see how in giving up type and shadow they secured the realities which these signified; to see how things visible and transitory were replaced by things unseen and eternal; to see how above the vanishing grace of the Levitical service rose in supreme and sovereign majesty the figure of the ascended Christ, Priest and King for ever, seated at the right hand of God, infinite in sympathy and power.

Now when we read the apostolic words, and picture to ourselves the sorrows which they illuminated—when we feel that in the portraiture of the perils of early believers we have the record

I. of true human struggles, and know that the essential elements of human discipline must always be the same—we cannot, I think, fail to recognise in the trials of the Hebrews of the first age an image of the peculiar trials by which we are beset; and so by their experience we may gain the assurance that for us also there is the promise of larger wisdom where they found it in
Hebr. xii. 27. wider views of Christ's Person and Work, that *the removal of those things that are shaken* is brought about in order *that those things which are not shaken may remain* in serener and simpler beauty.

If we look at the circumstances of the Hebrews a little more closely we shall notice that the severity of their trials came in a great degree from mistaken devoutness. They had determined, in obedience to traditional opinion, what Scripture should mean, and they found it hard to enter into its wider teaching. They had determined that institutions which were of Divine appointment must be permanent, and they found it hard to grasp the realities by which the forms of the older worship were replaced. They had determined that Christ's sovereignty should be openly vindicated by the victorious faith of God's people, and they found it hard to hold their belief firm against the general unbelief of their fellow-countrymen.

Now in these respects, we cannot, as I said, I.
fail to recognise that the difficulties of the Hebrews correspond with our own. For I am speaking now of the difficulties of those who hold to their first faith, and are yet conscious of shakings, changes, losses, of the removing of much which they formerly identified with it. Many among us, for example, tremble with a vague fear when they find that that "Divine Library," in the noble language of Jerome, which we call the Bible—"the Books"—"the Book"—cannot be summarily separated by a sharp, unquestionable line from the other literature with which it is connected; that the text and the interpretation of the constituent parts have not been kept free from corruptions and ambiguities which require the closest exercise of critical skill; that deductions have been habitually drawn from incidental modes of expression in Scripture which cannot be maintained in the light of that fuller knowledge of God's working which He has given us.

Others again find the historical problems raised by the study of the Bible carried into a wider region. They learn in the turmoil of action, and they learn in the silence of their own souls, that the Faith can no longer be isolated and fenced off from rude questionings as something

I. separate from common life. They perceive that they must bear, as they can, to see the deepest foundations of truth laid open and tested by impetuous inquirers; bear, as they can, to acknowledge once and again that formulas which, in earlier times, seemed to declare the Gospel adequately, no longer cover the facts of the world as they have been revealed to us in these later days.

And others have a more grievous trial still. As their view of the world is widened; as they come to understand better the capacities of humanity and the claims of Christ; as they are driven to compare the promises of the kingdom of God with the present fruits of its sway; as they feel that they cannot separate themselves from the race of which they are heirs; as they look upon the light, still after eighteen centuries
John i. 5. struggling (as it appears) against eclipse, their heart may well sink within them. We cannot wonder if such are tempted to ask with those of
2 Pet. iii. 4. old times, *Where is the promise of His coming?* or to listen with little more than the sad protest of a lonely trust to the bold assertions of those who say that the Faith has exhausted its power in dealing with the facts of an earlier and simpler civilization.

There is not, I believe, one who reads these words—not one who looks with calm, open eyes

upon the spectacle of the world and the nearer I.
vision of his own nature—who has not been stirred by the anxious thoughts which I have indicated, and asked how they shall be met, met not by a strong effort of overmastering will, but with that quiet confidence which is able to welcome every lesson of the discipline of God. And what then shall we say? How shall we escape the double danger which besets us, of hastily surrendering every position which is boldly challenged, or of rigidly refusing to consider arguments which tend to modify traditional opinion?

I do not doubt for one moment as to my answer. I bid those who are tempted to accept their trials with the frankest trust, as the conditions through which they will be brought to know God better. I have been forced by the peculiar circumstances of my work to regard from many sides the difficulties which beset our historic Faith. If I know by experience their significance and their gravity; if I readily allow that on many points I wish for fuller light; then I claim to be heard, when I say without reserve that I have found each region of anxious trial fruitful in blessing: that I have found my devout reverence for every word of the Bible quickened and deepened, when I have acknowledged that it demands the exercise of every faculty with which

I. I have been endowed, and, that as it touches the life of man at every point, it welcomes, for its fuller understanding, the help which comes from every gain of human knowledge; that I have found my absolute trust in the Gospel of the Word Incarnate confirmed with living power, when I have seen with growing clearness that no phrases of the schools can adequately express its substance, or do more than help men provisionally to realise some part of its relation to thought and action; when I have learnt through the researches of students in other fields to extend the famous words of the Roman dramatist, and say "*Christianus sum: nihil in rerum natura a me alienum puto*"—"I am a Christian; and therefore nothing in man and nothing in nature can fail to command the devotion of my reverent study"—; that I have found, even in the slow and fitful progress of the Church, which still does move forward, a spring of hope, when I turn, as I must turn from time to time, to take count of the unutterable evils of great cities, and great nations, and whole continents, which wait for atonement and redemption in the longsuffering and wisdom of God.   Yes, if, as I have endeavoured to shew, our trials, the trials of a new age, correspond with those of the Hebrews, the consolation which availed for them, avails for us also. We shall find

in due course, as they found, that all we are I.
required to surrender—child-like prepossessions, venerable types of opinion, partial and impatient hopes—is given back to us in a new revelation of Christ; that He is being brought nearer to us, and shewn in fresh glory, through the "fallings from us, vanishings of sense and earthly things" which we had been inclined to identify with Himself.

There is a picture with which we are all familiar, in which Christ seated in glory is represented as dispensing His gifts to the representatives of suffering humanity. From His hands the slave receives freedom and the sick health: the mourner finds rest in His sympathy, old men peace, children joy. "*Christus Consolator*" is indeed an image which touches every heart. But it is not the whole Gospel; it is not, I venture to think, the particular aspect of the Gospel which is offered by the Spirit of God to us now for our acknowledgment. Sin, suffering, sorrow, are not the ultimate facts of life. These are the work of an enemy; and the work of our God and Saviour lies deeper. The Creation stands behind Gen. i. 27.
the Fall, the counsel of the Father's love behind the self-assertion of man's wilfulness. And I believe that if we are to do our work we must learn to think, not only of the redemption of man,

I. but also of the accomplishment of the Divine purpose for all that God made. We must learn to
Eph. i. 10. think of that *summing up of all things in Christ,* in the phrase of St Paul, which crowns the last aspirations of physicist and historian with a final benediction. We must dare, in other words, to look beyond Christ the Consoler to Christ the Fulfiller. *Christus Consolator*—let us thank God for the revelation which leaves no trial of man unnoticed and unsoothed—leads us to *Christus Consummator.*

This thought of "Christ the Fulfiller" is, as it seems to me, the characteristic teaching of the Epistle to the Hebrews. The author of that marvellous book, speaking to the heart with a pathos to which the prophecy of Jeremiah offers the only parallel in the Bible, shews us in many ways how He through whom God made the world in all the rich variety of its growing life, has been
c. i. 2. appointed heir of all things; how He has fulfilled
c. ii. 9. the destiny of men in spite of the inroad of sin, and borne humanity to the throne of the Father;
cc. iv. 14 ff.; ix. 24. how in the plenitude of royal majesty He appears before God for those whose nature He has taken
cc. x. 19; xii. 22 ff. to Himself; how in Him we have present access to a spiritual society, in which earth and heaven, men and angels, are united in a glorious fellowship; how He has given us for our daily support

a covenant and a service, which transfigure the conditions of our conflict into sacraments of a higher order. I. cc. viii. 6; xiii. 10.

These, then, are the four thoughts which I wish to follow out in due succession. They meet our difficulties, as far as I can judge, with messages of widened hope, as they met the difficulties of the Hebrews. They enable us to realise with a personal and present conviction, that the Spirit of God is even now *taking of the things of Christ, and shewing them unto us;* that we too are living in an age of revelation, and called to listen to a Divine voice. John xvi. 14.

And if the thoughts seem strange to any, and removed from the familiar circle of religious reflection; if they require devout patience for their mastering; if they add an element of infinite interest to the commonest details of life, and therefore claim the tribute of complete self-surrender; let us remember that progress is still, as in the first age, the essence of our faith. We have to gather little by little the fruits of a victory in which Christ has overcome the world. The Hebrews were, as we have seen, in danger of apostasy, because they failed to go forward. And that we may be shielded from the like peril, the words which were spoken to them are spoken also to us: *let us be borne on to* Hebr. vi. 1.

I. *perfection*, not simply "let us go on," or even "let us press on," as if the advance depended on the vigour of our own effort, but "let us be borne on," "borne on" with that mighty influence which waits only for the acceptance of faith, that it may exert its sovereign sway, "borne on" by Him whose unseen arms are outstretched beneath the most weary and the weakest, "borne on" by Him who is the Way and the End of all human endeavour.

And as we are thus "borne on," as we yield ourselves, yield every gift of mind and body, of place and circumstance, yield all that we cherish
Rom. viii. 37. most tenderly, to the service of Him in Whom we are made more than conquerors, let us not fear that we shall lose the sense of the vastness of the Divine life in our glad consciousness of its immediate power. We assuredly shall not fail in reverent gratitude to our fathers for the inheritance which they have bequeathed to us, while we acknowledge that it is our duty to improve it. We shall not disparage the past, while we accept the inspiring responsibility of using to the uttermost the opportunities of the present. We shall cling with the simplest devotion to every article of our ancient Creed,
John xvii. 3; 1 John v. 20. while we believe, and act as believing, that *this is eternal life, that we may know*—know, as the

original word implies, with a knowledge which is I.
extended from generation to generation, and from day to day,—*the only true God and Jesus Christ.*

By the pursuit of this knowledge we come to recognise that the difficulties which press us most sorely are really the discipline through which God is teaching us: veiled promises of coming wisdom. We learn through the living lessons of our own experience that the eternal Gospel covers the facts of life, its sorrows, its needs, its joys, its wealth. Through every conflict the Truth is seen in the majesty of its growing vigour. Shakings, shakings not of the earth only but of the heaven, will come; but what then? We know this, that all that falls is taken away, *that those things which are not shaken may remain.*

II.

THE DESTINY OF MAN FULFILLED BY CHRIST THROUGH SUFFERING.

Not unto angels did he subject the world to come, whereof we speak. But one hath somewhere testified, saying, What is man, that thou art mindful of him? Or the son of man, that thou visitest him? Thou madest him a little lower than the angels; thou crownedst him with glory and honour, and didst set him over the works of thy hands: thou didst put all things in subjection under his feet. For in that he subjected all things unto him, he left nothing that is not subject to him. But now we see not yet all things subjected to him. But we behold him who hath been made a little lower than the angels, even Jesus, because of the suffering of death crowned with glory and honour, that by the grace of God he should taste death for every man. For it became him, for whom are all things, and through whom are all things, in bringing many sons unto glory, to make the author of their salvation perfect through sufferings.

HEBR. ii. 5—10.

THE DESTINY OF MAN FULFILLED BY CHRIST THROUGH SUFFERING.

THE form of the Epistle to the Hebrews is II.
unique among the writings of the New Testament. Without preface and without salutation the Apostolic author opens the innermost treasury of God, and *brings out things new and old.* He Matt. xiii. 52.
boldly re-affirms, with abrupt and majestic eloquence, the glory of the Christian Faith, by disclosing a fuller prospect of the person and the work of Christ. He shews how the manifold Hebr. i. 1—4.
lessons of earlier revelation were crowned by the coming of Him who was not servant but Son, the Maker and Heir of the world. He shews how the Hebr. i. 5—14.
angels, through whose ministry the Law was given, waited to do homage to Him, proclaimed King of the renovated order. He shews how our Hebr. ii. 1—4.
responsibility as Christians corresponds with the grandeur of the Truth which is placed within our reach. He shews how nothing is taken from the Hebr. ii. 5—18.
universal range of man's dominion, but—and this

II. is his peculiar message—that it must be reached, that it has been reached, through suffering.

So the writer of the Epistle met at once the central difficulty of the Hebrews. The Hebrews since they believed had been doomed outwardly to the bitterest disappointment. They had looked for a national welcome and they found themselves outcasts; for sovereignty, and they were the victims of popular outrage; for visible triumph, and, as the years went on, they were required to
Hebr. xi. 27. endure *as seeing*, through the thicker gathering gloom, *Him who is invisible.*

And he meets the difficulty by facing it in its fullest form. He passes from the sorrows of Israel to the sorrows of humanity. He quotes from the Psalter a description of the destiny, the position, the hope of man, which answers alike to the noblest aspiration and to the saddest experience. He sets forth the purpose of God in creation, and the failure of the creature, and then the triumph of Christ through suffering. In doing this he places in sharpest contrast what was promised to humanity and the actual condition of things. He abates nothing of the inspired estimate of man's nature, and honour, and sovereignty; but at the same time he claims no premature accomplishment of the promise as-
Hebr. ii. 8 f. sured to him. *We see not yet*, he confesses,

all things subjected to him. So far there is failure, II.
failure though the Christ has come. *But we* do *behold . . . Jesus*—the Son of man—*because of the suffering of death crowned with glory and honour.* There is the spring and the pattern of attainment, the interpretation of the shame and of the Passion of the Christ, which is for all time the interpretation of every grief that clouds the world, the pledge that the Divine counsel of love will not fail of fulfilment.

For, as we have already seen, the writer of the Epistle, when he met the difficulties of the Hebrews, meets difficulties which press sorely upon us. Time has not softened the sharpness of the impression which is made upon thoughtful spectators by the sight of the sorrows of life. If the contrast between man made *a little lower than angels*—nay literally *a little less than God*—and Ps. viii. 5 (R. V.).
man as man has made him, was startling at the time when the Apostle wrote, it has not grown less impressive since. Larger knowledge of man's capacities and of his growth, of his endowments and of his conquests, has only given intensity to the colours in which poets and moralists have portrayed the conflict in his nature and in his life. Whether we look within or without, we cannot refuse to acknowledge both the element of nobility in man which bears witness to

II. his Divine origin, and also the element of selfishness which betrays his falls. Every philosophy of humanity which leaves out of account the one or the other is shattered by experience. The loftiest enthusiasm leaves a place in its reconstruction of society where superstition may attach itself. Out of the darkest depths of crime not seldom flashes a light of self-sacrifice, like the
Luke xvi. 27 f. prayer of the rich man for his brethren when he was in torments, which shews that all is not lost. We cannot accept the theory of those who see around them nothing but the signs of unlimited progress towards perfection, or the theory of those who write a sentence of despair over the chequered scenes of life. We look, as the Psalmist looked, at the sun and the stars, with a sense which he could not have of the awful mysteries of the depths of night, but we refuse to accept space as a measure of being. We trace back, till thought fails, the long line of ages through which the earth was prepared to be our dwelling-place, but we refuse to accept time as a measure of the soul. We recognise without reserve the influence upon us of our ancestry and our environment, but we refuse to distrust the immediate consciousness of our personal responsibility. We do not hide from ourselves any of the evils which darken the face of the world, but we

do not dissemble our kindred with the worst and lowest, whose life enters into our lives at a thousand points. We acknowledge that *the whole creation groaneth and travaileth in pain together until now*, but we believe also that these travail pains prepare the joy of a new birth. We make no effort to cast off the riddles or the burdens of our earthly state, but we cling all the while to the highest thoughts which we have known as the signs of God's purpose for ourselves and for our fellow-men. We allow that man and men are uncrowned or discrowned in the midst of their domain, but we hold that they cannot put off the prerogatives of their birth. We ask, as prophet and apostle asked: *What,* O Lord, *is man that Thou art mindful of him? or the son of man that Thou visitest him?* without any expectation that we shall find an answer to the questions; but none the less we proclaim what we know, and confess that He is mindful of us, that He has visited us, that *the Word became flesh and tabernacled among us, full of grace and truth.*

II. Rom. viii. 22. John i. 14.

And indeed this Gospel reconciles the antagonisms of life. The fact of the Incarnation shews the possibilities of our nature as God made it. The fact of the Passion shews the issues of sin, which came from the self-assertion of the creature.

II. The fact of the Resurrection shews the triumph of love through death. Christ, in a word, fulfilled man's destiny, fellowship with God, by the way of sorrow; and the Divine voice appeals
Hebr. ii. 10; comp. c. vii. 26. to us to recognise the fitness of the road. *It became Him*—most marvellous phrase—*It became Him for whom are all things, and through whom are all things, in bringing many sons unto glory to make the Author of their salvation perfect through sufferings.*

When we ponder these words we shall all come to feel, I think, that they have a message for us on which we have not yet dwelt with the patient thought that it requires, though we greatly need its teaching. The currents of theological speculation have led us to consider the sufferings of Christ in relation to God as a propitiation for sin, rather than in relation to man as a discipline, a consummation of humanity. The two lines of reflection may be indeed, as I believe they are, more closely connected than we have at present been brought to acknowledge. I do not however wish now to discuss the propitiatory aspect of the sacrifice of Christ's life. It is enough for us to remember with devout thankful-
1 John ii. 2. ness that *Christ is the propitiation not for our sins only, but for the whole world,* without further attempting to define how His sacrifice was effi-

cacious. And we move on surer ground, II.
when we endeavour to regard that perfect sacrifice from the other side, as the hallowing of every power of man under the circumstances of a sin-stained world, as the revelation of the mystery of sorrow and pain. Of this truth the writer of the Epistle assumes that we are competent judges. He appeals to our natural sense of its 'fitness.' Again and again he presents the thought as the motive and the issue of the Incarnation. He shews that the Advent fulfilled the words of the Psalm: "*Lo! I am come to do Thy will, O Lord,*" c. x. 5 ff.
.... "*a body didst Thou prepare for me*"; and he describes the whole sum of the Lord's earthly work in a phrase which, if we can take it to our hearts, must become a transfiguring of life: *though* c. v. 8 f.
He was Son, He yet learned obedience by the things which He suffered, and having been made perfect—perfect by suffering—*He became to all that obey Him the Author of eternal salvation.*

Yes, Christ, *though He was Son,* and therefore endowed with right of access for Himself to the Father, being of one essence with the Father, for man's sake, as man, won the right of access to the throne of God for perfected humanity. *He learnt obedience,* not as if the lesson were forced upon Him by stern necessity, but by choosing, through insight into the Father's will, that self-surrender

II. even to the death upon the Cross which was required for the complete reconciliation of man with God. And so the absolute union of human nature, in its fullest maturity, with the Divine in the one Person of our Creator and Redeemer, was wrought out in the very school of life in which we are trained.

When once we grasp this truth the records of the Evangelists are filled with a new light. Every work of Christ is seen to be a sacrifice and a victory. The long years of obscure silence, the short season of conflict, are found to be alike a
John xvii. 19. commentary on the Lord's words, "*For their sakes I sanctify myself.*" And we come to understand how His deeds of power were deeds of sovereign sympathy; how the words in which Isaiah spoke of the Servant of the Lord, as
Is. liii. 4; Matt. viii. 17. Comp. John i. 29. "taking our infirmities and bearing our sicknesses," were indeed fulfilled when the Son of man healed the sick who came to Him healed them not by dispensing from His opulence a blessing which cost Him nothing, but by making His own the ill which He removed.

Dimly, feebly, imperfectly, we can see in this way how it *became God to make the Author of our salvation perfect through sufferings;* how every pain which answered to the Father's will, became to Him the occasion of a triumph, the disciplining

of some human power which needed to be brought II.
into God's service, the advance one degree farther
towards the Divine likeness to gain which man Gen. i. 26.
was made; how, in the actual condition of the world, His love and His righteousness were displayed in tenderer grace and grander authority through the gainsaying of enemies; how, in this sense, even within the range of our imagination,
He saw of the travail of His soul and was satisfied. Is. liii. 11.

Dimly, feebly, imperfectly we can see also how Christ, Himself perfected through suffering, has made known to us once for all the meaning, and the value of suffering; how He has interpreted it as a Divine discipline, the provision of a Father's love; how He has enabled us to perceive that at each step in the progress of life it is an opportunity; how He has left to us to realise "in Him"
little by little the virtue of His work; *to fill up* Col. i. 24.
on our part, in the language of St Paul, *that which is lacking of the afflictions of Christ* in our own sufferings, not as if His work were incomplete or our efforts meritorious, but as being living members of His Body through which He is pleased to manifest that which He has wrought for men.

For we shall observe that it was because He brought *many sons to glory,* that *it became God to make perfect through sufferings the Author of their*

II. *salvation.* The fitness lay in the correspondence between the outward circumstances of His life and of their lives. The way of the Lord is the way of His servants. He enlightened the path which they must tread, and shewed its end. And so it is that whenever the example of Christ is offered to us in Scripture for our imitation, it is
e. g. 1 Pet. ii. 21. His example in suffering. So far, in His strength, we can follow Him, learning obedience as He learned it, bringing our wills into conformity with the Father's will, and thereby attaining to a wider view of His counsel in which we can find rest and joy.

We must dare to face this solemn fact. For the most part we are tempted to look to the Gospel for the remission of the punishment of sins, and not for the remission of sins. But such a Gospel would be illusory. If the sin remains, punishment is the one hope of the sinner; if the sin is forgiven and the light of the Father's love falls upon the penitent, the punishment, which is seen as the expression of His righteous wisdom, is borne with gladness. Responsive love transfigures that which it bears. Pain loses its sting when it is mastered by a stronger passion. The true secret of happiness is not to escape toil and affliction, but to meet them with the faith that through them the destiny of man is fulfilled,

that through them we can even now reflect the II.
image of our Lord and be transformed into His 2 Cor. iii. 18.
likeness.

For the power of love is not limited by its personal effects. It goes out upon others with a healing virtue. Not only does the mother know no weariness in ministering to her child, but the sympathy of a friend can change the sorrow which it shares. So love kindles love; and, in the world such as we see it, suffering feeds the purifying flame. Was I not right then when I said that the thought of Christ perfected through suffering, does indeed bring light into the darkest places of the earth? In that light, suffering, if I may so speak, appears as the fuel of love. Up to a certain point we can clearly perceive how the vicissitudes, the sadnesses, the trials of life, become the springs of its tenderness and strength and beauty; how the stress of the campaign calls out the devotion of him whom we had only known as a self-indulgent lounger; how a cry of wrong stirs the spirit of a nation with one resolve; how a cry of agony is answered by the spontaneous confession of human kinsmanship; how the truest joys which we have experienced have come when we have had grace to enter most entirely into a sorrow not our own. And even where sight fails, the virtue of the

II. Lord's life made perfect through suffering guides us still. We know that not one day of His hidden discipline was fruitless. Each had its lesson of obedience; each marked a fresh advance in the consummation of manhood. So taught, we can feel how the lonely sufferer is still a fellow-worker with Him; how in the stillness of the night-watches a sleepless voice of intercession, unheard by man, but borne to God by a "surrendered soul," may bring strength to combatants wearied with a doubtful conflict; how
John iv. 37. the word "one soweth and another reapeth," may find a larger application than we have dreamed of, so that when we wake up we may be allowed to see that not one pang in the innumerable woes of men has been fruitless in purifying energy.

Looking then to Christ, Born, Crucified, Risen, Ascended, we can look also on the chequered scene of human life without dissembling one dark trait or abandoning one hope, and claim, in spite of every sign of present disorder, the promise of man's universal dominion as the watchword of our labour. *We see not yet all things subjected to Him; but we behold . . . Jesus because of the suffering of death crowned with glory and honour. . .* And again looking at the conditions of our own life, we can confess through the experience of quickened love that the Gospel justifies itself: that *it became Him, for whom are all things, and through whom are all things, in bringing many sons unto glory, to make the Author of their salvation perfect through sufferings.* II.

III.

THE KING PRIEST.

Having then a great high priest, who hath passed through the heavens, Jesus the Son of God, let us hold fast our confession. For we have not a high priest that cannot be touched with the feeling of our infirmities; but one that hath been in all points tempted like as we are, yet without sin. Let us therefore draw near with boldness unto the throne of grace, that we may receive mercy, and may find grace to help us in time of need.

HEBR. IV. 14—16.

For such a high priest became us, holy, guileless, undefiled, separated from sinners, and made higher than the heavens.

HEBR. VII. 26.

Now in the things which we are saying the chief point is this: We have such a high priest, who sat down on the right hand of the throne of the Majesty in the heavens.

HEBR. VIII. 1.

THE KING PRIEST.

NO thoughtful person can seriously regard the circumstances of his life without feeling the need of forgiveness and the need of strengthening. He looks back upon the past and he sees not only failures, but unnecessary failures. "He has done what he ought not to have done, and he has not done what he ought to have done." He looks forward to the future, and he sees that while the difficulties of duty do not grow less with added years, the freshness of enthusiasm fades away, and the temptation to accept a lower standard of action grows more powerful. Perhaps in the words of Hood's most touching lyric, he thinks "he's farther off from heaven Than when he was a boy." At any rate, he does feel that in himself he has not reached and cannot reach that for which he was born, that which the spirit of divine discontent within him, a discontent made keener by temporal success, still marks as his one goal of III.

III. peace. For when Augustine said, *Tu nos fecisti ad te, Domine, et inquietum est cor nostrum donec requiescat in te,*—"Thou, O Lord, hast made us for Thyself, and our heart is restless till it find rest in Thee"—he proclaimed a fact to which every soul bears witness in the silence of its self-communings. We know that we were made for God; we know that we have been separated from God; we know that we cannot acquiesce in the desolation of that divorce.

We know, I say, that we have been separated from God. The sense of this separation makes itself felt in two ways. When we reflect what God is and what we are, we shrink from His presence, and we confess that we are unworthy to do Him service. At the same time, by a splendid contradiction, we still seek instinctively for some way of access by which we may draw near to Him, and for some channel of grace through which our sin-stained tribute may be brought before His throne.

So it has been that men in every age have made priests for themselves, to stand between them and their God, to offer in some acceptable form the sacrifices which are the acknowledgment of sin, and the gifts which are the symbol of devotion. The institution of the priesthood has been misused, degraded, overlaid with terrible superstitions, but in its essence it corresponds

with the necessities of our nature. Therefore it III.
has been interpreted and fulfilled in the Bible. And we can yet learn much from the figures of the Levitical system in which the priesthood *of this* Hebr. ix. 1.
world was fashioned by the Spirit of God in a form of marvellous significance and beauty. The law of the priestly service in the Old Testament is indeed a vivid parable of the needs, the aim, the benediction of human life. Day by day, Num. xxviii. 3 ff.
morning and evening, the broad lessons of atonement and consecration were read with simple and solemn emphasis; and once in the year, on the Great Day of Atonement, "the Day," as it was Lev. xvi.
called, the lessons were set forth in detail with every accessory of majestic ritual, so that the simplest worshipper could hardly fail to take to himself with intelligent faith the warnings and the consolations of the august ceremonial. On that day, as will be remembered, the High Priest, after elaborate cleansings, for himself, for his family, and for the people, arrayed in white robes, entered, in the virtue of a surrendered life, into the dark chamber, which God was pleased to make His dwelling place, and offered incense in the golden censer, and sprinkled the blood, and uttered aloud, according to tradition, on that occasion only, the most sacred Name; and then, after completing the purification of the whole

III. Temple, he dismissed into the wilderness the scape-goat on which he had laid the sins of the people. On that day, though but for a passing moment, Israel in their representative appeared before the revealed presence of the Lord their God. On that day they received from Him most directly the assurance of forgiveness and
Hebr. iv. 16. blessing—*mercy and grace to help in time of need.*

Now we can, I think, all understand what must have been the consolation, the strength, the joy, with which that service inspired the faithful Jew; how it must have spoken peace in the name of Jehovah to the troubled conscience, and brought vigour to the trembling; how, as the passing weeks added weight to the burden of remembered sins, the people must have looked forward to the message brought again from the innermost sanctuary of Truth, that the divine compassion was as vast as their distress; how in the power of that visible pardon they would, within a few days, join in the Feast of Tabernacles, "the holiest and greatest" of all their festivals, and shew for a brief space the gladness of social life fulfilled by the gift and in the sight of God.

We can understand all this; and therefore, when we make the effort, we can understand what

the Hebrew Christians must have felt when they III.
found themselves at last excluded from all share in this consolation, this strength, this joy, which they had known from their childhood.

Here was a trial which reached to the very foundation of their spiritual life. It was not only that they were condemned to suffering; that might be a beneficent chastening of sons. But they seemed to be bereft of the appointed assurance, given in a form suited to the conditions of earth, that God was accessible to man.

This was a distress which called for a deep-reaching remedy; and the writer of the Epistle meets it as he meets all distress. He does not direct his readers as he might have done, and the fact calls for careful thought, to the outward institutions of the Christian society; he does not shew how provision had been made by the love of God to bring the power of the Gospel to bear on the whole range of human life, outward and inward; he does not point out how sacraments as revelations of the eternal go immeasurably beyond types which are prophecies of the future. He leads the Hebrews in their forlorn loneliness at once to Christ, to *Jesus, the son of God.* He Hebr. iv. 14.
recognises with tender sympathy, he alone we must notice of the apostolic writers, the grace and the splendour of the old order; he dwells with

III. reverent memory on the significance of the ritual which he had known; and then he shews how to the Christian every symbol had become a truth, every shadow a reality, every imaged hope a fact in a perfect human life; he shews how the sacrifice of Christ was efficacious for ever, "one act at once;" how the humanity of Christ was a new and living way to the Father; how on the divine throne placed above the opened heavens,
Hebr. vii. 16. was seated One who was Priest *according to the power of an indissoluble life.*

In doing this he carries forward the line of revelation which we have already considered. The work of Christ on earth was the preparation for His work in heaven.

He who fulfilled the destiny of man, under the conditions of the present world; He who interpreted the discipline of suffering; He who bore humanity through death to the presence of God—not as one man of men, but as the Head of the
Hebr. ii. 17. whole race—did all this *that He might be a merciful and faithful High Priest,* and that He might
Hebr. ii. 11. apply to those whom He was *not ashamed to call brethren,* the virtue of His Life and Passion, and reconcile in a final harmony the inexorable claims of law, and the infinite yearnings of love, a Priest and yet a King.

For indeed at first and at last the kingly and

princely offices cannot be kept apart. The combination which meets us in the simplest forms of society meets us again when humanity is seen to have reached its goal. The truth which is thus expressed lies deep in the facts of life. It answers to the connexion of the seen and the unseen. He who makes atonement must direct action. He who demands the complete service of every power must hallow the powers of which He claims the ministry. The ruler who consecrates, the priest who rules, must, in the words already quoted, be *merciful and faithful*; He must have absolute authority and perfect sympathy; authority that He may represent God to man, sympathy that He may represent man to God. And such is Christ made known to us, King and Priest, *Priest after the order of Melchisedek,* in whose mysterious person the old world on the edge of a new dispensation met and blessed the father of the faithful. Therefore the writer of the Epistle once again is able to appeal to the human conscience to justify the Gospel. Therefore he can say, when he has shewn what Christ is, *able to save to the uttermost* with royal power, *ever living to make intercession* with priestly compassion; *such a High Priest became us*—we with our poor faculties can see how He answers to our wants—*holy* in Himself, *guileless* among men,

Hebr. v. 10; vi. 20.

Hebr. vii. 1 ff.

Hebr. vii. 25 ff.

III. *undefiled* in a corrupt world, *separated from sinners* in the conflicts of this visible order, *and made higher than the heavens...a Son perfected for evermore.*

Yes, the apostolic words are true for us, true while there is one sin to vex the overburdened conscience, one struggle to strain the feeble will, *such a High Priest became us.* And it is well for us to turn again and again with reverent devotion to Him as we know, and that we may know better, our faults and our weakness.

We need not dwell long upon His authority. Son of God in His own essential nature, He vindicated His Sonship among men. He brought humanity at each stage of His advancing life into perfect fellowship with God, offering a perfect service as well as a perfect sacrifice, and then at
John xix. 34. last—most marvellous paradox—He offered Himself in death upon the cross, and living through death, His earthly work ended, He entered on the glory of His eternal priesthood, and *sat down on*
Hebr. viii. 1. *the right hand of God.*

cc. i. 3, 13; viii. 1; x. 12; xii. 2. That single phrase "*sat down on the right hand of God,*" on which the writer of the Epistle dwells with solemn emphasis, marks the unique dignity of the ascended Christ. Priests stand in their ministry; angels stand or fall prostrate before the Divine Majesty; but the Son shares the Father's

throne. As Priest, as Intercessor, He reigns still, III.
reigns in His glorified manhood.

There is our reassurance. Our Priest is King, and our King is Priest. *The Son of God* is also *Jesus*, the Son of man. His tender compassion is infinite even as His authority. We know now that what Ezekiel saw in a vision has become for Ezek. i. 26.
us a fact. We see by faith upon the sapphire throne not the shadowy likeness of a man, but One who is true man; One who was *made in all* Hebr. ii. 17.
things like unto His brethren; One who was *tempted in all things after our likeness;* One who Hebr. iv. 15.
has known the bitterness of every human trial, and who knows the secret of their use; One whose sympathy goes out to every suffering creature as if he were alone the object of His regard; One whose love kindles to responsive warmth the faintest spark of faith.

We can feel then how the Hebrews through their apparent loss were brought to an immeasurable gain, and how we may learn a little better through their example what our King-Priest is for us.

If human priests compassed with infirmity could inspire confidence in the worshipper, then Christ, if we will lift our eyes to Him, a thousand-fold more. Their compassion was necessarily Hebr. v. 1 ff.
limited by their experience, but His experience

III. covers the whole field of life; their gentle bearing was tempered by the consciousness of personal failure, but His breathes the invigorating spirit of perfect holiness. They knew the power of temptation in part by the sad lessons of failure; He knew it to the uttermost by perfect victory. They could see dimly through earth-born mists something of the real hideousness of evil; He saw it in the undimmed light of the Divine purity. And He is tenderest, not who has sinned, as is sometimes vainly thought, but who has known best the power of sin by overcoming it. His love is most watchful who has seen what wrong is in the eyes of God.

Can we not then boldly proclaim that here also the Gospel covers the facts of life, of our life? that in the prospect of the conflicts and defeats which sadden us, and which we dare not disguise or extenuate, *such a High Priest became us,* strong with the strength of God, compassionate with the affection of a friend?

Gen. xxxii. 24 ff. We must cling to both these truths, and wrestle with them, and win their blessing from them. We need the revelation of Christ's Majesty, and we need the revelation of Christ's Tenderness. We need more, I think, than we know, to come each one of us into the presence of the glorified Lord and rest in His light.

In this individual approach to the throne of grace lies for us severally the promise of the fulfilment of our destiny; But "earth's children cling to earth," and there are many among us who feel keenly the very trials which the Hebrews felt; who long for some visible system which shall "bring all heaven before their eyes," for some path to the divine presence along which they can walk by sight, for recurrent words of personal absolution from some human minister, for that which shall localise their centre of worship; who labour, often unconsciously, to make the earthly the measure of the spiritual; who shrink from the ennobling responsibility of striving with untiring effort to hold communion with the unseen and eternal; who turn back with regretful looks to the discipline and the helps of a childly age, when they are required to accept the graver duties of maturity; required to listen, as it were,
like Elijah on the lonely mountain, when the 1 K. xix. 12.
thunder of the earthquake is stilled and the violence of the fire is spent, for the still small voice.

These are not, I know, imaginary temptations; but if we are tried and disquieted by their assaults, the writer of the Epistle enables us to face them. He brings Christ near to us and he brings us near to Christ. He discloses the privileges to which

III. we are all admitted by the ascended Saviour. He gives an abiding application to the Lord's words, *He that hath seen Me hath seen the Father.* (John xiv. 9.) And he does this without hiding one dark trait in the prospect of life. The connexion in which the text stands gives it a startling force. The apostolic author has recalled without reserve, the sad history of Israel's failure. He has painted a vivid picture of the penetrating severity of the Divine judgment, and then, drawing an unexpected conclusion from this revelation of unbelief and weakness and retribution, he continues: (Hebr. iv. 14 ff.) *Having therefore a great High Priest who hath passed through the heavens, Jesus the Son of God, let us hold fast our confession. For we have not a High Priest that cannot be touched with the feeling of our infirmities; but one that hath been in all points tempted like as we are, yet without sin. Let us therefore draw near with boldness unto the throne of grace, that we may receive mercy and may find grace to help in time of need.*

Every word must go to the heart of those who have known what life is, an inexorable order capable of being transfigured by love. Every word has a practical force. Never was the charge to hold fast our confession more urgently needed. Never was the encouragement to come directly to Christ more fitted to still the griefs of failure, and

to nerve the misgivings of weakness. Never was III.
the twofold necessity of rising out of themselves without losing themselves more impressingly forced upon men by the contrast between their ideal and their attainment, their destiny and their position; never was the Spirit more openly claiming acceptance for growing Truth.

As then we have known a little of the power of our Faith; as we have felt the want of forgiveness and the want of support; as we have learnt a little more clearly with advancing years the grievousness of sin and the perils of life, *let us*, each in our place, *hold fast our confession.*

Let us draw near with boldness to the throne of grace—giving utterance to every feeling and every wish—*that we may receive mercy*—receive it as humble suppliants from the Lord's free love—*and may find*—find as unwearied searchers—*grace to help in time of need.*

That access is ever open to the foot of faith. That mercy is unfailing to the cry of penitence. That grace is inexhaustible to the servant who offers himself wholly to the Master's use.

IV.

THE UNIVERSAL SOCIETY.

Ye are come unto mount Zion, and unto the city of the living God, the heavenly Jerusalem, and to innumerable hosts of angels, to the general assembly and church of the firstborn who are enrolled in heaven, and to God the Judge of all, and to the spirits of just men made perfect, and to Jesus the mediator of a new covenant, and to the blood of sprinkling that speaketh better than that of Abel.

HEBR. XII. 22—24.

THE UNIVERSAL SOCIETY.

WE have seen that the solemn and consolatory lessons of the priestly service of the Old Testament, which were brought together in their highest form on the Day of Atonement, obtained their fulfilment in the work of Christ. We have seen that Christ realised in the victorious progress of a perfect life that absolute holiness, of which ceremonial cleansings were a figure; that He, uniting in one Person the offices of priest and victim, *through the eternal spirit, offered* the humanity which He had taken to Himself, a sacrifice well-pleasing to God upon the altar of the Cross, *not for the nation only,* but for the world; that through the grave, and through the heavens, He bore His own blood, the virtue of His Manhood given for men, to the immediate presence of God, pleading on our behalf for ever; that going infinitely beyond the privilege of intercession by that one entrance, He sat down IV. Hebr. ix. 14; xiii. 10. John xi. 52. Hebr. iv. 14.

IV. as Divine King on the Father's throne, crowning the ministry of priestly compassion with the glory of universal sovereignty.

So far the types of the Day of Atonement have been fulfilled, and far more than fulfilled; but the last scene in the august ceremonial of the day has not at present found its counterpart. Our High Priest has not yet returned from the heavenly sanctuary to reveal on earth the completeness of His work in visible triumph. Our position therefore is, in one sense, like that of the congregation of Israel gathered round the Holy Place, waiting with eager and beating hearts till their representative should come forth to bring again before their sight the fact of forgiveness and acceptance. We too are in an attitude of
Hebr. ii. 8. expectancy. *We see not yet all things subjected* to our Redeemer. Clouds and darkness are over the world which is His inheritance; and we look for Him, in the words of the Epistle, when He
Hebr. ix. 28. *shall appear a second time apart from sin, to them that wait for Him, unto salvation.*

This, I say, is one aspect of our position. We are in an attitude of expectancy; and in this respect it is of the utmost importance that we should keep our brightest hopes fresh, and neither dissemble the sorrows of life, nor surrender the
2 Cor. iv. 7. least of the Divine promises. *We walk by faith,*

not by sight. But the reality, the intensity, of our expectancy must not hide from us the reality of our attainment. If the appearance of Christ is future, fellowship with Him and with His people is present. *Ye are come,* the author of the Epistle writes, to men troubled by doubts, by divisions, by losses, by sufferings, as grievous as any which we have to bear, by shamelessness of triumphant vice to which Christendom offers no parallel, *Ye are come*—and not, "Ye shall come" —*unto mount Zion, and unto the city of the living God, the heavenly Jerusalem. . . . and to Jesus the Mediator of a new covenant. . . .* He writes, I repeat, "Ye are come," and not, "Ye shall come," and no blindness, no faithlessness, can alter the fact. IV. Hebr. xii. 22.

The Hebrews were, as we remember, in danger of forgetting the grandeur of their privilege under the stress of temporal affliction, and so the Apostle recalls the most memorable scene in their sacred history. He contrasts the beginnings of Judaism, and the beginnings of Christianity; the character of the old kingdom of God imaged in the circumstances of its foundation, and the character of the new kingdom made clear in its spiritual glory through tribulations and chastenings, that they might see what the Gospel was not as well as what it was. *Ye are not come,* he says, *unto*

IV. *a palpable and kindled fire, and unto blackness, and darkness, and tempest, and the sound of a trumpet, and the voice of words.* . . . Ye are not come, that is, like your forefathers, to an outward, earthly, elemental manifestation of the Divine Majesty, which appealed to the senses, and even where it was most intelligible and most human, struck those to whom it was given with overwhelming dread; *but ye are come unto mount Zion, and unto the city of the living God, the heavenly Jerusalem, and to innumerable hosts of angels, to the general assembly and church of the firstborn who are enrolled in heaven.* . . . Ye are come, come already, come even if God seems to hide Himself, to a Divine Presence nearer and more pervading than Moses knew, to an abiding communion realised in vital energy and not to a passing vision shewn in material forces, to a revelation marked, as the Apostle goes on to shew, not by threatening commands, but by means of reconciliation, inspiring not fear but love.

Now when we reflect upon the contrast, we shall be led to perceive that it could not fail to suggest thoughts of reassurance to the Hebrews. They were, it is true, shut out, irrevocably shut out, from the courts of the Temple, deprived of the friendship of those who claimed to be the children of the patriarchs and the prophets,

outcasts from the visible commonwealth of God. IV.
But what then? When they lost these earthly privileges which gave a transient satisfaction to their souls, they were taught even through their grief to gain a larger vision of the Divine action and of the Divine presence; to see through the typical splendours of the vanishing sanctuary, *the city that hath the foundations,* of which every Hebr. xi. 10.
institution of earth is a partial shadow; to see Hebr. xii. 1 f.
about them the great cloud of witnesses who proclaim that not one aspiration of faith has ever failed of attainment; to see on the right hand of the Father—that right hand which is everywhere—Him in whom all creation finds its unity and its life, Jesus, Son of man and Son of God, accessible to each believer; to see that Christianity is not an etherialised Judaism, but its spiritual antitype; that the heavenly Jerusalem is no material locality, but the realm of eternal truth; that the Christian society is not in essence an external organization, but a manifestation of the powers of the new life.

And for us this teaching has, I think, a still wider application. The spectacle of divided and rival Churches is as sad and far vaster than the spectacle of unbelieving Israel. It is hard for us to bear the prospect of Christendom rent into hostile fragments as it was hard for the

IV. Hebrews to bear the anathema of their countrymen. It is hard to look for peace, and to find a sword; to look for the concentration of every force of those who bear Christ's name in a common assault upon evil, and to find energies of thought and feeling and action weakened and wasted in misunderstandings, jealousies, and schisms; to look for the beauty of a visible unity of the
John xvii. 21. faithful which shall strike even those who are without with reverent awe, and to find our divisions a commonplace with mocking adversaries. It is hard; and if what we see were all, the trial would be intolerable. But what we see is not all: what we see is not even the dim image of that which is. The life which we feel, the life which we share, is more than the earthly materials by which it is at present sustained, more than the earthly vestures through which it is at present manifested. That is not most real which can be touched and measured, but that which struggles, as it were, to find imperfect expression through the veil of sense: that which to the All-seeing Eye gilds with the light of self-devotion acts that to us appear self-willed and miscalculated; that which to the All-hearing Ear joins in a full harmony words that to us sound fretful and impatient; that which fills our poor dull hearts with a love and sympathy

towards all the creatures of God, deeper than just hatred of sin, deeper than right condemnation of error, deeper than the circumstances of birth and place and temperament which kindle the friendships and sharpen the animosities of human intercourse. IV.

Yes, the unseen and the eternal is for all of us who confess Christ come, Christ coming in flesh, the ruling thought of life. To us also the words are spoken—*Ye are come unto mount Zion, and unto the city of the living God, the heavenly Jerusalem, and to innumerable hosts of angels, to the general assembly and church of the firstborn who are enrolled in heaven; and to the God of all as Judge, and to the spirits of just men made perfect, and to Jesus the Mediator of a new covenant, and to the blood of sprinkling which speaketh better than that of Abel.* 1 John iv. 2; 2 John 7.

Ye are come, that is, come though your way seems to be barred by inevitable obstacles, though your prospect seems to be closed by impenetrable gloom, to a scene of worship and a company of fellow-worshippers which no eye hath seen nor can see; ye are come to powers of the spiritual order which are able to bring assurance in the midst of the confusions, the uncertainties, the failures, by which you are wearied and perplexed; ye are come, in a word, to a dispensation, not

IV. earthly but heavenly, to a dispensation not of terror but of grace.

Each of these two characteristics of the Divine order to which we are admitted, that it is heavenly, and that it is gracious, has for us, as for the Hebrews, a message of encouragement.

If the outward were the measure of the Church of Christ, we might, as we have seen, well despair. But side by side with us, when we fondly think,
1 K. xix. 14, 18. like Elijah or Elisha's servant, that we stand
2 K. vi. 17. alone, are countless multitudes whom we know not, angels whom we have no power to discern, children of God whom we have not learnt to recognise. We have come to the kingdom of God, peopled with armies of angels and men working for us and with us because they are working for Him. And though we cannot grasp the fulness of the truth, and free ourselves from the fetters of sense, yet we can, in the light of the Incarnation, feel the fact of this unseen fellowship; we can feel that heaven has been re-opened to us by Christ; that the hosts who were separated from Israel at Sinai by the fire and the darkness are now joined with us under our Saviour King,
John i. 51. *ascending and descending upon the Son of man;* that no external tests are final in spiritual things; that while we are separated one from another by barriers which we dare not overpass, by differences

of opinion which we dare not conceal or extenuate, IV.
there still may be a deeper-lying bond in *righteous-* Rom. xiv.
ness, peace, and joy in the Holy Ghost, the apostolic 17.
notes of the kingdom of God, which nothing that is of earth can for ever overpower.

Such convictions are sufficient to bring a calm to the believer in the sad conflicts of a restless age, widely different from the blind complacency which is able to forget the larger sorrows of the world in the confidence of selfish security, and from the superficial indifference which regards diversities as trivial which for good or evil modify the temporal workings of faith. They enable us to preserve a true balance between the elements of our life. They teach us to maintain the grave, if limited, issues of the forms in which men receive the truth, and to vindicate for the Spirit perfect freedom and absolute sovereignty. They guard us from that deceitful impatience which is eager to anticipate the last results of the discipline of the world and gain outward unity by compromise, which is hasty to abandon treasures of our inheritance because we have forgotten or misunderstood their use. They inspire us with the ennobling hope that in the wisdom of God we shall become one, not by narrowing and defining the Faith which is committed to us, but by rising, through the help of the

IV. Spirit, to a worthier sense of its immeasurable grandeur.

And yet more than this: they quicken our common life with a vital apprehension of the powers of the unseen order; they break the tyranny of a one-sided materialism; they proclaim that a belief in natural law is essentially a belief in a present God; they take possession of a region of being which answers to the capacities of the soul; they encourage us to bring our ordinary thoughts and feelings into the light of our eternal destiny, and add to them that idea of incalculable issues which must belong to all that is human.

At the same time there is an element of awe in this revelation of the fulness of spiritual force active about us, of this association with invisible fellow-workers, of this communion with Him who
Hebr. xii. 29. *is a consuming fire.* And the writer of the Epistle does not shrink from dwelling on the sterner aspect of his teaching. He insists on the heavier responsibility which attaches to those who have larger knowledge. He calls for the exertion, the courage, the thoughtful endurance, the watchful purity, which correspond with the truths that he has laid open.

Life indeed is filled with awe. Its solemnity grows upon us. We may wish to remain children always, but we cannot. And here the Gospel meets the fears which spring out of the larger vision of our state. It is heavenly and it is gracious too. We have come not only to an order glorious with spiritual realities, but also to an order rich in provisions of mercy: *to the God of all as Judge, and to the spirits of just men made perfect, and to Jesus the Mediator of a new covenant, and to the blood of sprinkling which speaketh better than that of Abel.* The words teach us to look backward and to look forward, and to draw from the past and from the present the inspiration of faith. We look to those whose work is over, we see that judgment is a deliverance for surrendered souls, and that the work of Christ has brought perfection to His servants through the sufferings of earth. We look to those who are still pressed in the fight, and we see with them Jesus the Son of man, shewing in His own Person that God is their support, and applying to each the virtue of His life.

IV.

Hebr. xii. 23 f.

Once again then we are brought to Him, when our thoughts are turned to the widest mysteries of life. When we behold the depths of heaven opened about us, and the veil lifted from the living fulness of earth, He stands before our face—stands as He appeared to His first martyr—to welcome those who follow Him in hope within the sanctuary of the Divine Presence.

Acts vii. 56.

IV. Once again He is revealed to us as bringing the help which we need in view of the questions which are forced upon us by the circumstances in which we are placed. We have seen already that He has transfigured suffering by shewing that it is through suffering humanity is perfected. We have seen that He has consecrated a new and living way for us to God, by bearing our manhood to the throne of heaven. We see now that, when we regard the innumerable forms of being which crowd the spiritual temple, He is with us still, to assure us that there is a place for us in that august company and to prepare us for taking it.

Hebr. x. 20.

Once again He is revealed to us as communicating to His people of His own glory for the accomplishment of their destiny. He is the Firstborn, and He gathers round Him *a Church of the firstborn,* in which Divine family each member shares the highest privilege. "Cum pluribus," wrote an early commentator from the solitude of his French convent, "major erit beatitudo; ubi unusque de alio gaudebit sicut de seipso." Yes; "The bliss will be greater when more share it. In heaven each one will rejoice for his fellow as for himself."

Once again He is revealed to us as the Fulfiller —*Christus Consummator*—gathering into one and reconciling all things by the will of God.

And let no one think that such a revelation is fitted only to fill the fancy with splendid dreams. It is, I believe, intensely practical. He who leaves the unseen out of account deals as it were with a soulless world, with a mechanical structure of matter and force. But for the Christian all is law, and life, and love. He has *come unto mount Zion, and unto the city of the living God, the heavenly Jerusalem, and to innumerable hosts of angels, to the general assembly and Church of the firstborn who are enrolled in heaven . . . and to Jesus the Mediator of a new covenant. . . .* IV.

For him the wilderness, desolate to the bodily eye, is thronged with joyous ministers of God's will. For him no differences of earth can destroy the sense of kindred which springs from a common spiritual destiny.

What then, we are constrained to ask, is this revelation, what are these facts to us? Do they not meet the loneliness which has depressed us, the weakness which has often marred our efforts?

It must be so if God, in His love, open our eyes to behold the armies of light by which we are encircled; if He open our hearts to feel the strength of fellowship with every citizen of His kingdom.

V.

THE NEW COVENANT.

But now hath he obtained a ministry the more excellent, by how much also he is the mediator of a better covenant, which hath been enacted upon better promises.

HEBR. VIII. 6.

We have an altar, whereof they have no right to eat which serve the tabernacle.

HEBR. XIII. 10.

THE NEW COVENANT.

V.

THE attitude of a Christian is, as we have seen, twofold. It is an attitude of attainment, and an attitude of expectancy. He has been admitted to fellowship with the unseen order in the fulness of its infinite grandeur; and he is looking for the open manifestation of the victorious Presence of his Lord. This inspiring faith, this far-reaching hope, are bound together for each one of us by the obligation of personal duty. Each one of us has a work to do in that infinite kingdom of God which is opened to our entrance. Each one of us is charged in his measure to hasten the full (2 Pet. iii. 12.) revelation of its glory. We look through the temporal to the eternal. But for the present we have to live our little lives under the conditions of earth. We strive to gain the largest vision of the Divine counsels, to feel the intense reality of our connexion with the world about us, to watch in thought the stream of consequence

v. which flows from our actions; and then strengthened and humbled we go back as it were into the shrine of our own souls, and know that in that last depth of being we are alone with God. We are alone, and yet not alone, for there also Christ is with us, Christ the Fulfiller, to bring to its true perfection the fragment of service which answers to our powers. He not
Hebr. ix. 12; xii. 24. only bore His blood, the virtue of His offered life, into heaven for the salvation of the nature which He had taken to Himself, but He applies it personally to each believer on earth, to purify and to sustain, to begin and to complete that union with Himself for which man was made.

As the Hebrews grasped this truth which the Apostle set before them, they could not fail to find that what they had lost by their exclusion from the commonwealth of Israel was given back to them in fact, and not in figure. As Israelites they had rejoiced from early youth to enter the court of God's house; as Israelites, they had known in maturer age every consolation of the appointed sacrifices. But now, when they entered little by little into the meaning of the Gospel, they saw that they were become partakers
Hebr. viii. 6. in a better covenant than that made with their fathers, in a better sacrifice than those which the
Hebr. iii. 14; vi. 4. Law established, "partakers in Christ," "partakers

in the Holy Ghost." They were indeed, what Israel was designed to be, a nation of priests. The offering for the people's sin was for them given back as the support of life. v. Hebr. xiii. 10.

The lessons which were thus taught, taught most impressively through the symbols of the Old Testament, to men tried by the sorrows of the first age, are for us also. The individual soul as it turns to God requires to be assured of the personal right of approach to Him, and then of the power of continuous fellowship with Him. This assurance is given to us, in a form suited to the circumstances of our life, in the two Sacraments of the Gospel—the Sacrament of Incorporation, and the Sacrament of Support. In these we have, according to our need, the revelation of our union with Christ and the revelation of His impartment of Himself to us.

But we cannot fail to be struck by the way in which the writer of the Epistle deals with these Sacraments. We should have expected that he would contrast them in their significant forms with the typical Levitical rites to which they answered; that he would shew how even outwardly the Christian has in them far more sure seals of God's grace than the Jew; that he would point out that what was necessarily limited and local in the old dispensation had been made

v. universal in the new. As it is, he barely touches on the external element of the Christian Sacraments. The external element lies behind his teaching; but he strives above all things to fix the thoughts of his readers upon the ascended Christ who works through the Sacraments, lest they should rest in ritual observances, and faint or fail in the effort to gain a closer personal fellowship with Him.

There are, however, two remarkable passages which enable the student to perceive, as I have already indicated, the deep meaning of the Mystical Washing, and of the festal meal of the Eucharist. *Let us draw near*—near to the Holy place—the Apostle writes, *with a true heart in fulness of faith, having our hearts sprinkled from an evil conscience, and our body washed with pure water.* And again, *We have an altar, whereof they have no right to eat which serve the tabernacle.*

Hebr. x. 22.

Hebr. xiii. 10.

The first passage shews that by our covenant rite we are made not only a people of God, but also priests of God.

The second passage shews that while the sin-offering on the Day of Atonement was wholly consumed by fire, our common sin-offering is made our common peace-offering, our Eucharist, a Feast upon a Sacrifice.

Twice only in the Pentateuch is mention made of the sprinkling of the blood of sacrifices upon men; once at the solemn ratification of the covenant, when the people were united to the Lord; and once when Aaron and his sons were hallowed for the priesthood. In the latter case the sprinkling with blood was united with a washing with water. Here then we have the complete parallel with the words of the Epistle. To a Jew familiar with the Mosaic record, their meaning was distinct and decisive. They set forth that the Christian is made, as I said, not only a citizen of the Divine kingdom, but also a priest of God; that for him access to heaven is open; that he has boldness to offer the sacrifices of word and deed; that he accepts the duty of consecration.

V.

Ex. xxiv. 8.
Lev. viii. 23 f; 30; 6.

Hebr. xiii. 15 f.

The interpretation of the second passage which I have quoted has been disputed, but I think that the general sense is clear. The writer is meeting a difficulty found in the supposition that Christians had not what the Jews had. *We have*, he replies, *an altar*, an altar with a victim, for the two are not separated, *whereof they have no right to eat who serve the tabernacle.* We have, that is, more, infinitely more, than the Law allowed to those who ministered to figures of the eternal truth. We have Christ crucified, Christ upon the Cross,

v. a victim and an altar, a victim who suffered for the world without the camp, and who then, marvel of marvels, gave and gives Himself for ever as the support of His people in a Holy Eucharist. No priest in old time ever tasted such an offering. But He who died for us lives for us. He who bore our sins gives us of the fulness of His strength. And, to go one step further, on Him and in Him we can bring to God the sacrifice of ourselves.

So then, we repeat, our covenant rite, our Baptism, brings us into a personal relation to Christ. No one stands between the believer and the Lord. Our Sacrificial Feast, our Eucharist, offers to us the virtue of Christ's life and death, His Flesh and Blood, for the strengthening and cleansing of our bodies and souls.

Let us look at these thoughts a little more closely.

As baptized, confirmed Christians, priests of God, we can come directly to the Father. No earthly symbol, no mortal representative, intervenes any longer as the necessary means through which we may draw near.

As baptized, confirmed Christians, priests of God, we can offer up to Him a sacrifice of praise and active love, the natural fruit of hearts touched
John xv. 7. with His grace. No fear checks the thanksgiving

which is the echo of His word. No weakness v.
stays the effort which is the answer to His summons.

As baptized, confirmed Christians, priests of God, we acknowledge that we are *holy, partakers of a heavenly calling,* dedicated to God without reserve, *bearing branded* upon us, in St Paul's vivid image, *the marks of Jesus,* as bondmen devoted to His perpetual service. Hebr. iii. 1. Gal. vi. 17.

But while this is so; while nothing can alter the responsibility which is laid upon each soul, and which we have voluntarily acknowledged; while we must severally, as if there were none other, draw near to God and bring Him the offering of ourselves, and acknowledge the debt which is as large as life; our approach, our sacrifice, our dedication, are all *in Christ.* Not one step, not one act, not one confession, can be made without Him. *We are become partakers of Christ.* Hebr. iii. 14. That is the gift of God. And while the Epistle recognizes, as we have seen, the priesthood of Christians, this human priesthood falls almost out of sight before the supreme fact of the priesthood of Christ. Our common priestly work is done only through Him. *Through Him we offer up a sacrifice of praise to God continually.* Hebr. xiii. 15. Our will makes it our own. His co-operation makes it acceptable.

V. *We are become partakers of Christ, if,* it is
Hebr. iii. 14. added, *we hold fast the beginning of our confidence firm unto the end.* A Divine fact, such is the paradox of life, is made dependent on human endeavour. We can see then how the institution of the Eucharist meets the sad sense of infirmity and failure. Our covenant rite cannot from its nature ever be repeated. But we know how often and how grievously we have fallen short of our obligation. Is the covenant then, we are driven to ask, fatally broken? When the fear rises before us, we recall, almost regretfully, the provisions which men have made, with or without the sanction of God, to bring, through sacrifice, peace to the troubled conscience. While we do so, the Apostle lifts up our thoughts to the Lord, Crucified, Risen, Seated at the right hand of the Father, and in the light of that
Hebr. xiii. 8. vision of *Jesus Christ, the same yesterday and to-day, yea, and for ever,* we can say triumphantly, *We have an altar.* All that the consolatory ceremonial of the Old Dispensation accomplished for Israel, all that men have sought to make clear to themselves by vain speculations and worldly forms, is ours in spiritual and abiding simplicity. *We have an altar* wherein the truths which were represented by the sacrificial system of the Law are realised in a living verity. *We have an altar,*

whereon we can lay "ourselves, our souls and bodies," a reasonable service. v.

Once again then we are brought to Christ the Fulfiller—*Christus Consummator*—in whom each believer finds the root and the accomplishment of his individual destiny.

So, we have reached the limit which we set to ourselves. We have dared to look upon great trials in the light of the Epistle to the Hebrews, and we have seen that the help which availed the Hebrews in the first age is sufficient for us.

We have looked upon suffering, and we have seen that by the will of God suffering is for fallen man the way to perfection. We cannot indeed, with our feeble sight, discern how this or that sorrow and shame contributes to the end; but disciplined in patience, we can leave in the Father's hands the fulfilment of His own law which we have recognised, and for our part labour to hasten that issue.

We have looked upon failure and weakness, and we have seen that Christ, as He accomplished the destiny of man on earth, pleads the cause of man in heaven with unfailing compassion and absolute sovereignty, uniting the offices of priest and king, perfect man and perfect God.

We have looked upon the sad spectacle of

v. divided Christendom, and we have seen that by the Ascension of Christ we are brought into a spiritual fellowship, in which the powers of heaven and earth are united, a fellowship transcending every test of sense; and from the contemplation of notes of that universal communion, we have learnt to keep hope fresh while we guard with watchful reverence the convictions which separate us in the sphere of visible work.

We have looked upon the chequered course of the individual life, and we have seen that for each one of us is provided that objective assurance of our right of approach to God which is the solid foundation of religion, that objective assurance of the renewed gift of Christ's flesh and blood, which is able to sustain and to purify us in the effort to reach His likeness.

At every prospect of great trial, as we dwelt patiently upon it, we have seen the figure of Christ to rise above the darkness—of Christ the Fulfiller—not only to give comfort, but to enlarge hope, not only to support the sufferer under the pressure of transitory affliction, but to shew to the believing soul that, in a world such as this,

> "Failure is but a triumph's evidence
> For the fulness of the days."

And we have seen all this, so far as we have been allowed to see it, by entering a little more

closely than is commonly done into the difficulties v.
of a troubled congregation of the apostolic times. Thus we have found that the words of the inspired writer who guided the Hebrews to higher things, speak to us with the directness and the power of life. We have found on a narrow field of inquiry what the Bible is: an interpretation of the eternal, intelligible to every man through all time in the Acts ii. 5 ff.
language in which he was born. We have found that nothing has befallen us which our fathers have not borne victoriously in other shapes and made fruitful in blessing. We have found, I think, that to those who will raise their eyes to Christ the Fulfiller, the Revelation of the John xiv. 9.
Father, made known to us more completely from John xiv. 26.
generation to generation by the Holy Spirit, nothing in human experience can come as an unwelcome surprise. He, Son of man, Son of God, will bear, He has borne, though we see it not through the mist of days and years, all things to their goal, *Christus Consummator*.

Such thoughts carry with them a grave, a noble responsibility. The character of a generation is moulded by personal character. And if we have considered some of the temptations of the first Christians; if we know a little of the terrible environment of evil by which they were encircled;

V. we must not, as we too often do, forget how they conquered the world. It was not by any despairing withdrawal from city and market; not by any proud isolation in selfish security; not by any impatient violence; but by the winning influence of gracious faith, they mastered the family, the school, the empire. They were a living Gospel, a message of God's good-will to those with whom they toiled and suffered. Pure among the self-indulgent, loving among the factious, tender among the ruthless, meek among the vainglorious, firm in faith amidst the shaking of nations, joyous in hope amidst the sorrows of a corrupt society, they revealed to men their true destiny and shewed that it could be attained. They appealed boldly to the awakened conscience as the advocate of their claims. They taught as believing that He who had stirred their heart with a great desire would assuredly satisfy it.

They offered not in word but in deed, the ideal of spiritual devotion, and "the soul naturally Christian," turned to it, as the flower turns to the light, drew from it, as the flower draws from the light, the richness of perfect beauty.

Yes; that was the secret of their success; and it is the secret of our success. The words are true now as they were when addressed by Zechariah to the poor remnant of Jews struggling to rebuild

their outward temple: *Not by might, nor by power,* v.
but by My Spirit, saith the Lord of hosts. Not Zech. iv. 6.
first by material change, not by intellectual culture,
but by spiritual sympathy will our work be done.
Let us take to ourselves the charge of our Epistle,
the counsel of Divine fellowship—fellowship with
God and man, fellowship with man in God. *Let* Hebr. iv. 16.
us draw near unto the throne of grace. . . . Let us Hebr. x. 23.
hold fast the confession of our hope. . . . Let us Hebr. x. 24.
consider one another to provoke unto love and good
works, and it shall not be long said that the
victories of faith are ended.

CHRISTUS CONSUMMATOR. II.

ASPECTS OF THE INCARNATION.

But Mary kept all these sayings, pondering them in her heart.

ST LUKE ii. 19.

THE INCARNATION A SUBJECT FOR DEVOUT STUDY.

THERE is no grander passage in Greek litera- I.
ture than that in which Plato describes how the contemplation of absolute justice, temperance, and knowledge is the sustenance of the divine nature. There are times of high festival, he says, in the world above, when the gods in solemn procession mount to the topmost vault of heaven, and taking their place upon its dome, gaze over the infinite depths of perfect Truth. This spectacle supports the fulness of their being. Nor are they, he continues, alone in the enjoyment of the magnificent vision: all the souls that can and will follow in their train. Such of these as are able to gain the fair prospect and keep it before their eyes, while the spheres revolve, remain in the possession of supreme joy. The rest baffled, wearied, maimed, sink down to earth and are embodied as men. Henceforward he adds, their condition in this lower life depends

Phædr. p. 246 D.

I. upon their past apprehension of the Truth. Their human existence is a striving upwards toward the glory which they have once seen. They live still, so far as they really live, by the recollection of that which has filled them with a noble passion.

The life of man is thus according to the highest thought of Greek philosophy remembered Truth. Such an intuition of noble souls found its confirmation and fulfilment in the Presence
John xvii. 3. and in the word of the Lord: *This is,* He says, *the life eternal—This* is the life, and not This is its condition, or its foundation, or its portal, or its preparation—*This is the life eternal, that they may know*—know, such is the force of the word, with a knowledge widening from hour to hour under the discipline of experience and opportunity—*Thee the only true God, and Him whom Thou didst send, even Jesus Christ.*

Yes: the life of man is the knowledge of God, the contemplation of Him Who is the Truth. That is the message of Christ. But this knowledge lives and moves. It is not a dead thing embalmed once for all in phrases of the school which can be committed to memory. It is offered ever fresh as time advances for reverent study in the Person of the Word Incarnate. The surest knowledge once gained cannot supersede the necessity of unwearied, unceasing, inquiry.

No one can absolve himself from the duty of spiritual thought. I.

The words which I have chosen for a text present the duty to us with almost startling force. The Mother of the Lord had received that direct, personal, living, revelation of the purpose and the working of God which none other could have: she had acknowledged in the familiar strain of the *Magnificat* the salvation which He had prepared through her for His people: she might well seem to have been lifted far above the necessity of any later teaching; but when the simple shepherds told their story, a faint echo as we might think of what she knew, she *kept all these things pondering them in her heart*, if haply they might shew a little more of the great mystery of which she was the minister: she kept them waiting and learning during that long thirty years of silence, waiting and learning during that brief time of open labour, from the first words at the Marriage Feast to the last words from the Cross. Luke i. 46 ff. Luke ii. 19. Luke iii. 23. John ii. 4; xix. 26.

And shall we, brethren, when we think on such an example, we with our restless and distracted lives, with our feeble and imperfect grasp on Truth, be contented to repeat with indolent assent a traditional confession? Can we suppose that the highest knowledge and the highest knowledge alone is to be gained without effort, without

I. preparation, without discipline, and by a simple act of memory? Must the eye and the hand of the artist be trained through long years to discern and to portray subtle harmonies of form and colour while that spiritual faculty by which we enter on the unseen may be safely left unexercised till some sudden emergency calls it into play? Is it credible that the law of our nature, which adds capacity to experience and joy to quest, is suddenly suspended when we reach the loftiest field of man's activity?

To ask such questions, as if the answer could be doubtful, is a reproach to our intelligence. To ask them in the silence of the soul, as seeking to feel their application, is a salutary discipline. We lose more than we know because we do not habitually meditate on the grandeur of our Creed. True it is that the vision which Plato imagined has been given to us as an abiding possession under the conditions of earth. But that the divine revelation may become the master force of our whole being we must dwell upon it. We must regard that most solemn Presence of the
John xiv. 9. Father in Christ with lingering, loving, gaze till each detail grows significant to us according to the place which we occupy in the order of Providence. We must see it with our own eyes and not another's, thankful for every help to better in-

sight which we have inherited or enjoyed, but rest- I.
ing neither in the treasure of truth which we have received nor in our own past gains. The sum of human experience grows visibly from age to age; the sum of personal experience grows visibly from year to year; and the Truth ought to find fresh fulfilment in every fact of life.

In this respect we must, I fear, condemn ourselves of negligence. For if, as I assume, the Gospel touches us, yet we do not labour further to trace the lines of its infinite expansion. So it comes to pass that we fail to gain a growing sense of the obligations which it imposes, of the prerogatives which it confirms, of the strength which it brings, strength, prerogatives, obligations, limited only by our capacity to apprehend and appropriate them, for *without controversy great is the mystery*— 1 Tim. iii. 16.
the revelation—*of godliness*—not a formula or a statement but a living Person, *even He Who was manifested in the flesh, justified in the spirit, seen of angels, preached among the nations, believed on in the world, received up in glory.*

Yes: great, inexpressibly great, is *the mystery* of our faith; and at this season when the transcendent mystery, the transcendent revelation, is once again specially brought before us, I desire, as I may be enabled, to touch upon some points in which it appears to me to concern us most nearly

I. as men, as fallen men, as men placed in a world of marvellous complexity, as men busied with a life of endless issues, to shew in other words a little more fully how, as indicated last summer, a patient contemplation of the Person and work of Christ will enable us to meet with confidence and joy the trials of a new age.

But before we enter on the consideration of these four aspects of the Incarnation I wish by way of introduction to indicate now the spirit, the aim, the blessing of the work in which I invite you to help me by your thoughts, your sympathy, your prayers.

1. *The spirit.* In all that concerns the soul we know only when we love, and we know as we
Hebr. xi. 6. love. *He who comes to God,* we read, *must believe that He is, and that He is a rewarder of them that diligently seek Him.* And more than this: he must believe that every thought of tender service and self-surrender, every aspiration towards a conscious fellowship with all created things, every striving towards a truer unity, by which we are stirred, corresponds in its essence with the infinite perfection of Him in Whose image we are made. He must interpret all that is noblest in the soul as a foreshadowing of Divine realities. Thus Love springs out of Faith,
Hebr. xi. 1. and is supported by it. Faith enables us to enter

on the unseen, to give reality to the fabrics of I.
hope. And Love, borne by faith, dimly sensible of its power under the limitations of earth, rises into that spiritual realm, and knows that all things are possible to the love of God.

We shall then contemplate the signs of this immeasurable love with the humblest reverence, untroubled if we are unable to fit them together perfectly under the forms of human thought. Nay rather we shall rejoice that we cannot do so. Unreconciled antitheses are prophecies and promises of a larger future: 'our failure is but a triumph's evidence for the fulness of the days.' If our Faith could find a complete and consistent expression here it would be condemned. It would not cover all the facts of life. The forms of thought belong to this world only. The truth of life, like man, like Christ Who is Himself the Truth, belongs to two worlds. It is not simply the determination of physical phenomena, but the interpretation of the relation of man to nature and to God. The heart has its own office in the search for it. Not with the under- Rom. x. 10.
standing, not with the reason, but with the heart man believeth; and if ever our view becomes clouded: if a thick darkness hides Him towards Whom we strain our eyes: we shall recall for our warning and for our chastening, humbled and yet

I. sustained by hope, the benediction which tells us
Matt. v. 8. that *the pure in heart shall see God.*

2. This then will be our spirit, love illuminated by faith, attested by the heart. And it follows at once that our aim will be vital and not merely intellectual. We shall not strive to gain any completeness of technical definition on the doctrine of the Incarnation. We acknowledge indeed that outlines are a necessity for man's representation of the truth of things; but they are a concession to his weakness and a symbol of it. There is no outline in nature, and no form of words can adequately express a spiritual reality. The soul uses the outline, the formula, as an occasion, an impulse, a help; but it brings from its own treasure that which quickens them. And in this work the soul of the simplest, the most untutored, is at no disadvantage. Its chief instrument of spiritual progress is not knowledge but love.

So we shall look upon the Incarnation, the greatest conceivable thought, the greatest conceivable fact, not that we may bring it within the range of our present powers, not that we may measure it by standards of this world, but that we may learn from it a little more of the awful grandeur of life, that by its help we may behold once again that halo of infinity about common

things which seems to have vanished away, that 1.
thinking on the phrase *the Word became flesh* we John i. 14.
may feel that in, beneath, beyond, the objects which we see and taste and handle is a Divine Presence, that lifting up our eyes to the Lord in glory we may know that phenomena are not ends, but signs only of that which is spiritually discerned. And, while we confess that clearness of vision cannot be gained when we turn towards such an object except by the loss of that which is characteristic of it, as we look at the sun shorn of its glory through a darkened glass or through the thick mists of earth, it will be our joy to place ourselves in that atmosphere of light which transfigures all that it falls upon.

3. This will be our aim; and no one can have watched the tendencies of modern thought without seeing that it answers to one of our sorest needs. We are on the point of losing the sense of the spiritual, the eternal, as a present reality, as the only reality. Thought is not all: conduct is not all: life is unspeakably impoverished if it is unhallowed by the sanctities of reverence and worship.

And, if we have felt one touch of the spirit which should animate our contemplation of Christ Born, Crucified, Ascended, for us; if we have realised one least fragment of the end to which

I. our work is directed, we shall know what the blessing is: know what it is to see with faint and trembling eyes depth below depth opening in the poor and dull surface of the earth; to see flashes of great hope shoot across the weary trivialities of business and pleasure; to see active about us, in the face of every scheme of selfish ambition,
Hebr. vi. 5. *powers of the age to come;* to see in the struggles of the forlorn and distressed fragments of the life which 'the poor man' Christ Jesus lived; to see over all the inequalities of the world, its terrible contrasts, its desolating crimes, its pride, its lust, its cruelty, one overarching sign of God's purpose
Gen. x. 13. of redemption, broad as the sky and bright as the sunshine; to see in the Gospel a revelation of love powerful even now to give a foretaste of the unity of creation, powerful hereafter to realise it.

But, some will say, this blessing of faith, even in its fullest power, still leaves unremoved the evil, the sorrow, the suffering, the sin: the sordid cares of want, the reckless indulgence of wealth. True: but it leaves them only as one element in life, the most obvious, the most oppressive, but not the most enduring or the most powerful. It is when the physical order is held to be all, that life appears and must appear to be hopeless. As it is we can wait. We have found God in the world; found Him not in an Eden from

which we are banished, but in our world, taking I.
to Himself our infirmities and sicknesses; and it Matt. viii. 17.
is enough to remember that we have found Him. We see little: but He sees all.

We can therefore as we reflect on the Incarnation discern again 'the glory which hath passed from earth' without disguising one dark trait. We can recover with more than its first freshness a sense of Divine beauty about us. And we need the lesson in many ways. We need it, as I have said, from the dominant forms of current thought, and we need it from the conditions of life. As years go on there is great danger lest we should lose the ennobling faculty of wonder. We are occupied with small cares and they become the measure of our universe. Failures depress our faith; and disappointments dull our hope. Then this great spectacle of sovereign love rises before us, and the common things of earth are again touched with a heavenly light and become to us figures of the divine. Then wonder grows with knowledge; and though knowledge itself cannot satisfy, it can lift the soul to God by disclosing the infinite unknown.

At the same time the vision which elevates, soothes and calms. Differences of earth vanish in its presence. And if it be true that great duties and little souls do not go well together; it is no

I. less true that little thoughts do not suit little duties. It is in the fulfilment of simple routine that we need more than anywhere the quickening influence of the highest thought: and this the truth of the Incarnation, an eternal, an abiding truth, is able to bring to every Christian. Life may for a moment seem to be poor, and mean and commonplace, but when the reflection of this glory falls upon it, our wavering faith can alone dim its brightness.

So it is that we gain the final sense of the correspondence of the Gospel with the powers, the circumstances, the needs of man: so we rejoice to recognise the truth which we could not have discovered: so we find that our human language is not false, and our human aspirations are not illusory: so we place over all that is fleeting in form and transitory in its presentment the consecration of an eternal destiny.

The issue will not be gained at once. But each effort to interpret the signs of the Divine working will leave us stronger for new endeavours. Each space of quiet thought will bring us power of deeper vision. 'We have ourselves,' as it has been well said, 'as we use ourselves.' And just as our minds wither and waste if they are engrossed by sordid cares, so the thought of God in Christ enlarges and purifies every faculty which is occupied with it and lends something of its own I. nobility to the poorest heart which gives it a welcome.

But we must never forget the inexorable law of God's love. He gives *grace for grace.* He gives John i. 16. as His gifts are turned to service. He claims that we should be His fellow-workers. We could 1 Cor. iii. 9. imagine no loftier title; and no lower title would answer to the purpose of our creation. We were made to attain to the Divine likeness: made, that Gen. i. 26. is, as we can now see, to realise each in the narrow sphere of our fragmentary lives, each according to the measure of our ability, the fact of the Incarnation, to live in the light of that vision of absolute truth which has been opened to us, to live by the growth of that knowledge of God which He places within our reach through the fulfilment of daily duties.

To us also the Christ has been given. Luke ii. 11, 16, 19.

To us also the message of the angels has been made known.

To us also the sign of the Saviour has been fufilled.

Happy are we—then only happy—if we *keep all these things and ponder them in our hearts.*

II.

THE INCARNATION AND THE CREATION.

[He] made known unto us the mystery of his will, according to his good pleasure which he purposed in him unto a dispensation of the fulness of the times, to sum up all things in Christ, the things in the heavens, and the things upon the earth. EPH. I. 9.

THE INCARNATION AND THE CREATION.

THE conception which we form of God neces- II.
sarily determines the view which we form of the world and of life. This principle holds true even when we recognise most fully that our growing knowledge of the world and of life quickens and enlarges our conception of God. What then we ask characterises the Christian conception of God? To such a question we answer at once that it is determined by the fact of the Incarnation. *In the beginning was the Word, and* John i. 1, 14.
the Word was with God, and the Word was God... and the Word became flesh. This great mystery, this great revelation, is for us the *light* Ps. xxxvi. 9.
in which we shall see light. It is evidently inexhaustible in its teachings. It cannot be completely interpreted by any one race, or by any one age. As a fact of life it must become more and more intelligible as experience and inquiry reveal to us more completely the circumstances and conditions of life. Each fresh result won by

II. patient research into the constitution of our finite nature and of our sensible environment, helps us to understand a little better that truth which we have received, and therefore to apply it with a little greater force to the problems of the world.

In this respect it falls out that we can draw strength and instruction from our very trials. It is through difficulties fearlessly met that we are led to wider knowledge. We condemn ourselves to dead ignorance if we refuse to take account of them. In the order of Providence it comes to pass (may I not say it comes to pass by necessity?) that difficulties mark the direction of progress. It is obvious that the answer cannot be understood or effectively shaped till the question has been sharply put. A new requirement evokes unexpectedly a latent force. Hence it has happened in former times that the Truth has been found to satisfy needs which had made themselves felt in sadness and fear. The Faith which is in a Life, which is a Life, has been proved again and again to live itself, and to bring within its range larger fields of thought and larger promises of hope. And as it has been, so it will be still. The feelings, the desires, the movements of an age—of our own age—are not wholly in error. They are the manifestations,

often troubled and obscured by man's selfishness, II.
of a Divine will. Through these, as we believe, God is leading us by His Spirit, sent in the Name John xiv. 26. of His Son, to find a fuller meaning in the Creed which our fathers have transmitted to us to use in the busy fields of action and not to hide in Luke xix. 20. the barren security of a treasure-house.

We inquire therefore without mistrust whether there is any tendency of our own times which seems likely to suggest to us fruitful questionings. For my own part I find such a tendency in that striving after some kind of unity which has been stirred in many directions by a novel sense of our connexion one with another, and of our connexion with the material world. No one can doubt the power of this fascinating and generous impulse. No one can overlook its perils. Influential teachers persuade us on the one side to follow after the unity of Naturalism, which limits all knowledge to phenomena bound together by an inexorable sequence: on the other side, to lull ourselves to rest in the unity of Pantheism, which presents all things indifferently as the manifestation of one essence alone truly existent.

Such fictitious unities, however, can never bring peace. They take no account of our consciousness of responsibility, incompleteness, disharmony:

II. they take no real account of death. But if they are in themselves illusory, they do, I believe, fulfil the office which I have assigned to the spirit of the age. They direct us to aspects of the Incarnation which have not yet become the heritage of the Church, to visions of great hope through which we shall be enabled to meet the temper of doubt among us, which is at once formidable by its sincerity and significant by its form.

They direct us, I repeat, to unrecognised aspects of the Incarnation. For it is no disloyalty to the past to maintain that the view of the Incarnation which was gained in the 4th or 5th or 13th or 16th century was not final. Our fathers by the teaching of the Holy Spirit saw the Truth, but they did not see all the Truth. And it is, I think, impossible to look at modern writings without perceiving that the teaching on Christ's Person which is current in the most reverent schools falls short in many ways of the living fulness of the Bible. At one time the logical development of His true divinity leaves room only for a shadow of manhood, as unsubstantial as the phantom which already Hier. *Dial. adv. Lcf.* 23. usurped His place when in a familiar phrase His blood was still fresh in Palestine. At another time the loving portraiture of His true humanity places Him before us as a man among men, as one of many, as a part among parts; and not, according to His own self-chosen title, as the Son of man in Whom all the separate endowments of sex, and race and age co-exist in absolute harmony. In both ways we fail to grasp the promise of unity which lies in the true view of His Person. For in Holy Scripture He is shewn to stand essentially in some ineffable yet real connexion with all finite being. In Him, and through Him, and unto Him were all things made. He is the 'first-born,' 'the beginning' of all creation. Man was formed in His image; and in Him men find their consummation. The forces of Nature, so to speak, are revealed to us in the Bible as gathered together and crowned in man, and the diversities of men as gathered together and crowned in the Son of man; and so we are encouraged to look forward to the end, to a unity of which every imaginary unity on earth is a phantom or a symbol, when the will of the Father shall be accomplished and He shall *sum up all things in Christ*—all things and not simply all persons—both *the things in the heavens and the things upon the earth.*

II.

Col. i. 16.

Eph. i. 10.

If now we endeavour to determine the ultimate cause of the defectiveness of the modern teaching on the Person of Christ of which I have spoken, we shall find it, I believe, most plainly shewn in

II. the prevalent opinion as to the ground of the Incarnation. The Incarnation is commonly made to depend upon the Fall. And the whole tenour of revelation, as I conceive, leads us to regard the Incarnation as inherently involved in the Creation. The first Gospel is not the word of consolation: *The seed of the woman shall bruise the serpent's head,* but the word of the Divine counsel, *Let us make man in our image, after our likeness,* followed by the word of its initial accomplishment, *So God created man in His own image: in the image of God created He him.*

Gen. iii. 15.

Gen. i. 26, f.

In this august declaration of God's purpose and God's work we have set before us, clear beyond controversy, the primal endowment and the final goal of humanity. We are taught that man received, received inalienably as man, a fitness for gaining, through growth and discipline and continuous benediction, union with God. God's image was given to him that he might gain God's likeness. This original capacity of man was the measure of the love of God for His creature. Sin could not increase it: nothing less than personal union with God could fulfil it. The fitness and the necessity of the Incarnation exist therefore from the moment when man was made. The Incarnation, in other words, when we use the term in the most general sense,

apart from every thought of suffering and hu- II.
miliation, corresponds with the perfection of man as he was constituted at first, and not merely with the restoration of man who had missed his end. *Homo particeps Dei*—Man made partaker of God—is the satisfaction, the only possible satisfaction of *Homo capax Dei*—Man capable of receiving God. The marvel is that the purpose of creation was wrought out in spite of that wilful self-assertion of the creature which might have seemed to have fatally thwarted it.

Brethren, if you have in any degree followed me—and the thoughts which I have desired to suggest are rather strange and unfamiliar than intrinsically difficult—if you have felt, however dimly, what this Gospel of Creation is, I do not fear that you will think that I have directed your attention to fantastic or idle speculations. When a thousand hearts wait for some voice of encouragement, who would dare to beguile them with subtle fancies? Nay, rather, it is because the truth on which I have touched, the truth on which I pray you to meditate, seems to me to be intensely practical that I have striven to set it before you. For me at least the thought of the predestined humanity of the Eternal Word, the Son of God, as the archetype of humanity, throws light, growing light, upon some of those points of the Faith,

II. where many of us feel the darkness to be most oppressive.

It throws light upon the most solemn mystery of the Being of God. It helps us to understand how finite being was so prepared as to convey to a creature formed in the image of God a knowledge of God's nature and will, and thus to fit him to become a living and conscious shrine of His glory. It keeps God near to us in the fulness of our whole constitution. It teaches us to welcome and to use the imperfect conclusions of that Naturalism which offers a partial homage to the majestic progress of the physical order. It confirms the splendid visions which lend an unreal beauty to Pantheism by pointing to the
1 Cor. xv. 28. end when *God shall be all in all.*

It throws light upon the broken and chequered sum of human existence. It helps us to understand how the scattered fragments in which man's potential endowments have hitherto been realised combine to form a whole. There is a law, there is a Head from the first. There is no absolute separation of men in the complex variety of their functions. Men, so to speak, furnish the manifold elements through which (in the language
Eph. i. 23. of St Paul) a body of Christ is shaped; just as the world furnishes the elements through which man himself finds expression for his character.

It throws light on the conception of personality. II.
It helps us to understand how the self-assertion of the finite is sin and death; and how the complete self-surrender of love preserves and fulfils that which is truly individual, by delivering it from the weakness of isolation, by consecrating it to common service, by incorporating it in Him Who is *the* John xiv. 6.
Life. Thus directed we can see that all the differences of men, so far as they correspond with a true growth, contribute to the manifestation of the infinite perfection of the Son of man.

It throws light upon the connexion of man and nature. It helps us to understand how every discovery which encourages us to see an order in the unfolding of all things confirms the teaching of revelation on the Divine method and the Divine end: how the division, the differentiation of parts—call it as we will,—which culminates in man, points forward to a unity as well as backward: how the restoration of unity to mankind carries with it the restoration of unity to finite being.

It throws light, yet once again, upon the mystery of the future. It helps us to understand how that existence to which we look forward is not a mere indefinite continuance of divided lives, in which each one dwells apart, but some higher
type of a common life: a life in Christ: a life felt Gal. iii. 28.

II. in the fulness of personal fruition to be His life to which all in due measure offer that which is theirs: a life which thrills through each least member of the spiritual body with the intense and untiring joy of an absolute harmony.

It throws light, as I hope to shew next Sunday, upon the deep truths of the Atonement, upon the fulfilment of the destiny of man fallen. But not to enter on this subject now, I cannot but think that the idea of 'the Gospel of Creation' has already been shewn to be fruitful in great thoughts in relation to man as he was made by God. We welcome it, we keep it in our hearts, we ponder it; and little by little there takes shape before us a vision of the unity of nature in man, and of the unity of men in Christ, which satisfies desires that at present shew themselves importunately urgent. As we look and look, sending our souls with unwearied, unsatisfied delight through the infinities of time and space, there is, if I may so express myself, offered for our contemplation first an unfolding through the Divine creative love, and then an ingathering, an infolding, through the Divine perfective (or, as it is in fact, redemptive) love. We see, inscribed upon the age-long annals in which the prophetic history of the world and of humanity has been written,
Rom. xi. 36. the sentence of inextinguishable hope, 'From

God unto God.' We see when we look back upon II. the manifestation of the Divine plan that the order which we trace—nature, humanity, Christ—corresponds inversely with our earnest expectation of its fulfilment—Christ, the sons of God, Rom. viii. 18 ff. nature. We see, in short, while we thus regard the universe, as we must do, under the limitation of succession, from first to last a supreme harmony underlying all things which even sin cannot destroy. As yet, it is true, *we see* only *in part, through a glass, in a riddle,* but 1 Cor. xiii. 12. under this aspect we do see enough to make labour hopeful, to make thought consistent, and to bring every object which we perceive or feel within the scope of love.

How can it be otherwise? We all know how the astronomers of the middle ages were baffled by continually increasing perplexities as long as they endeavoured to refer the motions of the heavenly bodies to a central earth. When once the sun was taken for the centre all became clear, and the irregularities which remained proved the fertile source of later discoveries. So it is with Theology. Looking to the Incarnation as the crown of Creation we have found the true centre of the system in which we are set to work, even God and not man, love and not sin, the Creation which was the expression of the Father's

II. will, and not the Fall which was alien from it. Under the action of that central force of the Divine love the Incarnation reveals to us the essential possibilities and endowments of each separate life. It lifts us out of ourselves, above ourselves, that so we may find our truest selves in Him, Who has come to us that we may
Col. i. 16. come to Him, for Whom we were made and Who for us *became flesh.* In this double truth, which is one truth, we have in the face of things seen and temporal the test and the pledge of the eternal. All that truly *is* is the gift of God, summed up in His first and last gift of Himself.

With bowed heads and open hearts may we offer ourselves—we can do no more and we dare do no less—to the action of His love in and for which He created us. For us the nobility of freedom lies in the sense of dependence. For us the fulness of strength lies in the simplicity of Faith. We gaze for an instant on the Majesty within the veil that we may go forth
Ps. civ. 23. again into the world, *to our work and to our labour*, and still bear about with us the strong
Heb. vi. 5; xii. 2. assurance that the powers of the heavenly order are placed within our reach; that above the clouds and darkness which beset our path He is throned Who has borne our nature to the right hand of

God; that *in many parts and in many fashions,* II. Heb. i. 1.
through sufferings and chastisements, the Divine purpose is being fulfilled; that behind the veils of sense, which perplex and distract us, burns the serene glory of the Divine Presence; that beyond the spectacle of failures and conflicts which flow from selfishness, glows the prospect of a holy unity passing knowledge—a holy unity which shall hereafter crown and fulfil creation as one revelation of Infinite Love, when the Father's will is accomplished and He has *summed up all things in Christ, the things in the heavens and the things upon earth.*

III.

THE INCARNATION AND THE FALL.

It was the good pleasure of the Father that in Him should all the fulness dwell; and through Him to reconcile all things unto Himself, having made peace through the blood of His Cross; through Him, I say, whether things upon the earth, or things in the heavens.

COL. I. 19, 20.

THE INCARNATION AND THE FALL.

WE have seen already that the Divine record of Creation is indeed a Gospel, a revelation of the purpose of God's love for humanity. We have seen that the order of finite being is, as it is made known to us, fitted to be a manifestation of points in the character of God, leading up to the manifestation of Himself. We have seen that man was made capable of union with God, and that the possession of that capacity as a Divine endowment implies a promise of its satisfaction. We have seen that if, with our weak and disordered powers, we endeavour now to imagine what would have been the normal course of unfallen humanity towards its glorious goal, we must think of the happy and complete realisation of every potential energy of our nature through the discipline of a life relatively perfect, though fragmentary; for so the Divine likeness would have found fulfilment in III.

III. many parts: so at last the parts would have found unity in Him in Whose image man was made. We have seen that the conceivableness of the Incarnation lies in the thought of what man was originally made, and not in what he became through his self-assertion. We have seen that this Gospel of Creation is able to illuminate dark mysteries of the present and of the future, to disclose new depths for our contemplation in the nature of God and in the nature of man, to open dim foregleams of a unity which passes all understanding.

But while our eyes rest on the splendid vision, we are forced to ask whether it is indeed for us: whether we have not lost our birthright and our blessing beyond recall: whether the destiny of man can still be accomplished when he instinctively shrinks from Him in Whose Presence is life?

We all, I say, ask such questions when we regard the contradictions in our souls.

For everyone recognises in himself the two conflicting truths which are expressed in the narrative of the Fall: the power of evil and the prerogative of personal responsibility. There is we feel a 'baseness in our blood,' and we feel also that we have embodied the corruption 'by our fault, by our own fault, by our own great fault.'

The tendency indeed is our inheritance, but we have made the issues our own by deed, we are actually, and we know ourselves to be, guilty, enthralled, alienated from God. We look around us, and we see the double sentence of our own consciences written on a larger scale in the crimes and judgments of classes and nations, in the deeds of selfish violence which betray a common taint, and in the clear, unquestioning appeal of suffering souls to the majesty of a violated law. III.

What shall we say then? Is there for sinful men, for sinful humanity, forgiveness, redemption, reconciliation: a forgiveness which not only remits the debt but also removes the consequences which the debt has impressed upon the character: a redemption which not only rescues the captive from his oppressor but also inspires him with the vigour of freedom: a reconciliation which not only withdraws the barrier against the outflow of the love of God, but also opens the frozen springs of love in man? Or, is the evil which we see and feel irremediable?

We have heard indeed and we have dwelt with wonder on the primal purpose of God *to sum up* Eph. i. 10.
all things in Christ. But is that all? if so, we ask again, how can this purpose apply to us, being what we are? St. Paul seems to have

III. asked himself the same question; and he has answered it for us. *It was,* he says, *the good*
Col. i. 19 f. *pleasure of the Father through [The Son of His Love] to reconcile all things unto Himself, having made peace through the blood of His cross.* It was the purpose of God 'to reconcile' and not only 'to sum up'; 'to reconcile all things through Christ', by the efficacy of His action, and not only 'to sum up all things in Christ' by the embracing energy of His Nature; to *make peace* where confusion and conflict had found entrance; *to make peace by blood,* by the outpouring of a consecrated life given for the life of the world. Sin, in other words, did not alter the Divine purpose, but it modified the mode of its fulfilment.

In part we can understand this. Man did not
Gen. ix. 9. lose the image of God by the Fall. His essential nature still remained capable of union with God, but it was burdened and hampered. The Word therefore could still become flesh, but if in His infinite compassion He was pleased to realise this fellowship of the Divine and human, He took to Himself naturally, if we may so speak, humanity with its immeasurable obligations, life with its untold temptations and sorrows. In this there is nothing arbitrary, nothing which is not illustrated by universal experience, nothing which is not in accordance with the actual constitution

of the world. By becoming man the Word accepted the uttermost consequences of human existence: by becoming the Son of man, the Head, the representative of the race, He embraced them in their widest range. III.

In part, I repeat, we can understand this. We can understand how Christ—the Word become flesh—could suffer.

But some one will say, 'True: but if we allow that Christ could and did suffer: if we allow that men are bound one to another by the consequences of descent and the effects of intercourse: that they were so made as to rejoice and to weep together: that this is true socially and individually, true of states and of citizens: if we allow that Christ, by becoming man, entered on the accumulated heritage of human woes of His own will; yet my chief difficulty is untouched. How can another's suffering avail for my offence? How can punishment be at once vicarious and just? And perhaps he will add, 'I fairly claim an answer to my question. God did not refuse to accept the pleading of Abraham, which was based upon the human apprehension of righteousness; and He will not refuse to listen to our inquiry to-day; when we too say, *Shall not the Judge of all the earth do right?*' Gen. xviii. 25.

Yes, brethren, I at once admit that this, which

III. is indeed the question of questions for us, ought to be met. And when I said last Sunday that it is through our difficulties honestly stated and faced that God is pleased to guide us to fuller truth: when I said that under this aspect the characteristic thoughts of an age become articulate voices through the living interpretation of the Spirit; I was thinking not least of this question. For of all the directions in which the tendency towards unity, of which I spoke, has found expression, that which has led to the apprehension of social unity is perhaps the most fertile in suggestions for our own needs. Fifty years ago the term 'solidarity' and the idea which it conveys were alike strange or unknown. We had not apprehended in any living way that we are, as St Paul
Rom. xii. 5. says, literally *members one of another*, as men and nations. It was then fashionable to regard a state as an aggregation of individuals bound together by considerations of interest or pleasure. But we have now learnt in some degree, and we are learning better from year to year, that the family and not the individual is the unit of human life: that the nation is a larger family: that humanity is the ultimate family: that in all these the fundamental relations represented by parents, brothers and sisters, children, repeat themselves on different scales and offer final types

of order and progress: that we and our fathers and our posterity have been and must be born sons and citizens, heirs and stewards of wealth, physical, moral, spiritual, which no isolated effort could have accumulated; that the family, the nation, the race, are living wholes which cannot be broken up by any effort of individual will. We have learnt, in some degree, and we are learning better from year to year, to keep at the same time the humblest sense of our dependence and the liveliest sense of our liberty: to realise as a moral power the feeling of the unbroken continuity of life through the past and the present and the future: to acknowledge not only the necessity but also the blessing of suffering for others: to feel that St. Paul has revealed the power and the limit of sympathy when he tells us in the same paragraph: *Bear ye one another's burdens...and each man shall bear his own load.* (Gal. vi. 2, 5.) Yes: love can lighten the weight of the suffering which it cannot remove: it can transform what it cannot destroy. We have learnt, that is, in some degree, and are learning better from year to year, the one thought which, as far as I can see, makes it possible to believe the Gospel in its fulness, and not to close the eyes upon the facts of the world, the miseries of an African war, the burden of an Indian Empire.

III. Taught in this great school of domestic, national, human fellowship, we are coming to understand, as we could not do before, that sin affects not the individual only but the race, and that the just consequences of sin in every form answer to a law of holy love, that they include, as we regard them in parts, the ideas of reparation, of chastisement, of cleansing, which to our eyes are realised in parts slowly and in unexpected ways: to understand that in the conduct of our disordered life suffering contributes to the hallowing of man and of men: to understand that to noble and pure souls some imperfect yet real power of restoration is given, proportioned to their knowledge and their sympathy, and their
Hebr. v. 2. holiness—to their capacity for entering into the hearts of the ignorant, the weak and the erring, and for calling out in them the response of penitent devotion: to understand that in the unity of
Matt. viii. 17. the body it is possible for one member to take away the infirmity and disease of another by taking them to himself.

Taught in this great school we are coming to understand why the human instinct has always rejoiced in the stories of uncalculating self-devotion which brighten the annals of every people: why our hearts respond to the words of a Chinese king, contemporary with Jacob, who said to his people,

'When guilt is found anywhere in you who occupy 'the myriad regions, let it rest on me the One 'man'; and faithful to his prayer said again, when a human victim was demanded to avert a drought, 'If a man must be the victim, I will be he:[1]' why we do not think lives wasted which are offered in heroic prodigality to witness to a great principle: why the blood of martyrs is indeed seed, not idly spilt upon the ground, but made the vital source of a teeming harvest: we are coming to understand, in a word, what is the true meaning of that phrase 'vicarious suffering' which has brought at other times sad perplexity to anxious minds; how it excludes everything that is arbitrary, fictitious, unnatural, external in human relationships: how it expresses the highest energy of love which takes a friend's sorrows into the loving heart and taking them by God's grace transfigures them, satisfying every claim of righteousness, justifying every instinct of hope, quickening the spirit of self-surrender, offering within the sphere of common life a faint image of forgiveness, of redemption, of reconciliation. III.

So we are brought back to our great question, Can there be just forgiveness, redemption, reconciliation for sin? So I think we are prepared to

[1] Sacred Books of the East: *The Shu king: The announcement of Thang*, p. 91, and note.

III. answer it. We have found that the idea of the unity of humanity which underlies the Bible is brought home to us in daily intercourse: we have found that 'suffering is the fuel of love', the means of its perfecting, purifying action alike on him who suffers and on him for whom the suffering is borne: we have found that the measure of love's restorative efficacy in common human intercourse lies in knowledge, sympathy, holiness. Let then the knowledge be complete: let the sympathy reach to every creature: let the holiness be absolute: and there is provision for the atonement of fallen humanity; there is a propitiation for sins co-extensive with their presence; there is a force of all most prevailing to kindle the activity of Faith.

Each of these conditions was satisfied when *the*
John i. 14. *Word became flesh*; and now we can see how the Gospel of Creation meets our misgivings. Christ the Son of God, the Son of man, took to Himself a nature which from the first it was His good pleasure to crown. In Him every scattered fragment of manhood found its proper Head. Not one wrong through all its sad development was outside His penetrating knowledge. Not one least sorrow was alien from His spontaneous sympathy. Not one proud boast of self-sufficiency could maintain itself in the burning light of His

holiness. In Him men were able to recognise the harmonious maturity of every human endowment. In Him each man was able to recognise the consecration of his peculiar gift. In Him every single personality finds its true self. III.

Now we can see, even if it be in a riddle, a little more of the meaning of the Incarnation. Christ fulfilled perfectly the destiny of man, fulfilled through suffering the destiny of man fallen, realising at every stage and through death itself union with God: there lies for the whole race in Him the promise of forgiveness. Christ bore to the uttermost, even to the Cross, the consequences of human sin, and gave His blood to men as the power of a new life: there lies for the whole race the means of redemption. Christ shewed the Father's love with such persuasiveness of tender mercy as to move every awakened conscience to glad self-surrender: there lies for the whole race the potency of reconciliation.

And in all this there is nothing which offends the most delicate susceptibility of natural righteousness, nothing which does not find an anticipating welcome in the homage which is joyously rendered to self-sacrifice, nothing which does not find prophetic foreshadowing in the beneficent influence which the devotion of one man exer-

III. cises over the hearts of others, to inspire and to chasten.

Now therefore at last we can see how the mystery of Redemption corresponds to the mystery
Rom. v. 15. of the Fall. *If by the trespass of the one the many died, much more*—'much more'—*did the grace of God and the gift by the grace of the one man Jesus Christ abound unto the many.* On the one side we deplore our corruption; and we confess our guilt. On the other side we see in Christ the perfection of that towards which we strain, a perfection which He offers to us. God grant that we may take it by the faith which realises our fellowship with Him. For forgiveness, redemption, reconciliation, are not blessings which Christ bestows apart from Himself, but in Himself: in the humanity which He has created afresh and cleanses by His blood.

Oh, my friends, what an inexhaustible motive for labour lies in the revelation of one humanity, one in Creation, one in Redemption, one potentially in Christ. We cannot, if we would, gain our happiness alone: we cannot be saved alone. There is a wonderful Indian legend which tells how a Buddhist saint had reached by successive lives of sacrifice the stage next to Nirvâna. At that point he could by one effort of will obtain for himself eternal and untroubled calm. But when the decision had to be made he set aside the tempting prize, and chose rather to live again in the world while conflict could bear fruit. 'Not,' he said, 'till the last soul on every earth and in every hell has found peace can I enter on my rest.'

Do we not feel the Christian truth, which is enshrined in the splendid story? Not for ourselves only, as some peculiar and private blessing, is the Gospel given, the Gospel of Creation, the Gospel of the Word Incarnate. It is for the world; and it is laid upon us, upon each one of us, to realise what Christ has wrought for men, to claim for Him the fruits of His victory. We look upon the terrible spectacle of remediable evils thronging about us on every side: we look upon the Cross which has been made before our eyes an altar and a throne: we look upon the apostolic words which interpret the Father's purpose *to reconcile all things unto Himself through* the Son of His love. And our hearts accept the message of the will of God, as when from the great host at Clermont one voice welcomed the call to the first Crusade, and we too say, welcoming the call to fulfil Christ's triumph, 'It is the will of God.' That old call was to win by force of arms, through violence and desolation and slaughter, an empty sepulchre: the call which we hear is to win

III. by patience and love, through self-devotion and sacrifice, the living Body of Christ, the Church of redeemed humanity which He has *purchased*
Acts xx. 28. *with His own blood.* 'Deus vult! Deus vult.' 'It is the will of God.'

IV.

THE INCARNATION AND NATURE.

For the earnest expectation of the creation waiteth for the revealing of the sons of God....For we know that the whole creation groaneth and travaileth in pain together until now.

ROM. VIII. 19, 22.

THE INCARNATION AND NATURE.

IT was my object last Sunday to shew how one IV.
of the most characteristic thoughts of our age, that of the living membership of man with man and of nation with nation, the thought of the solidarity of humanity, which we have ourselves seen to take shape among us and to enter into popular aspirations, illuminates two of the greatest mysteries of our Faith, the mystery of the Fall and the mystery of the Atonement: how it throws light upon the meaning of suffering and upon the power of love: how it reconciles the instinct which affirms the absolute supremacy of righteousness, and the instinct which rejoices in the triumphs of self-devotion: how it gives to us in a form which the heart can embrace that conception of a common human life, in which the sense of corruption and the sense of responsibility, the acknowledgment of the fulfilment of man's

IV. destiny and the power of personally appropriating the virtue of Christ's work, are brought together in a vital harmony: how it offers to us a motive for labour which is able to consecrate every faculty and a spring of encouragement which is sufficient to refresh every fainting heart: how it inspires us to write over the wavering expression of the noblest ambition by which we have ever been stirred, of the loftiest hope to which we have ever reached forward, the sentence of Divine assurance, 'It is the will of God.'

All this seems to me to follow, to follow necessarily, from bringing the truth of the union of man with man, which great modern teachers have made known to us, into connexion with the central fact of the Incarnation. But the same masters have taught us also another truth. They have enabled us to realise, with a vividness impossible in earlier times, not only our union one with another but also our common union with nature. By this work they have doubled our debt to them, though for a time they seemed to have effaced the landmarks of man's heritage. They have in the end moved us to enter with surer trust a little further into the depths of the Scriptural doctrine of Creation, to welcome as sober truth the language which claims the
Ps. cxlviii. 9. service of life from *mountains and all hills,*

fruitful trees and all cedars, to find that in all that is truly human, in all that is eternal, the thoughts of the Written Word, if we go back to it with faithful, loving, humble, hearts, are ever beyond and before us, quickening us with grander aspirations, strengthening us with larger hopes, embracing in their wider range the last results which have been won by others from the study of the world.

Man then, I assume, is bound as closely on one side to earth and the creatures of earth as he is bound on the other side to heaven. So he appears in the Bible as the crown and king of Nature. He is neither above nor separated from the other works of God. Like a true king he delights in fellowship with his subjects. His isolation from the realm committed to him is a doctrine of heathen philosophy and not of Judaism or of Christianity. In revelation no less than in science man is the representative of Creation who gathers up into himself and combines in the most perfect form the various manifestations of life and being which are seen dispersed tentatively, as it were, through other orders.

This fact, when once it is admitted, can be used and has been used in two opposite ways. Some have found in it the occasion for degrading

IV. man to the level of their superficial estimate of the material world. Others, with a wider hope, have seen in the relation of matter to man indications, prophecies, promises, of some larger life than we have yet been able to conceive.

There can be no doubt to which alternative observation and inquiry are rapidly converging. 'Under one of its aspects,' writes Mr Herbert Spencer in his most recent volume, 'scientific progress is a gradual transfiguration of Nature. Where ordinary perception saw perfect simplicity it reveals great complexity; where there appeared absolute inertness it discloses intense activity; and in what appears mere vacancy it finds a marvellous play of forces...The conception to which [the explorer of Nature] tends is much less that of a Universe of dead matter than that of a Universe everywhere alive...'

Such a calm and solemn summary of the latest results of unbiassed research helps us, I repeat, to understand the words of St Paul in
Rom. viii. 19. which he tells us that *the earnest expectation of the Creation waiteth for the revealing of the sons of God...for we know that the whole Creation groaneth and travaileth in pain together until now*, words which stand alone in the Bible as a plain enunciation of facts of overwhelming magnificence: words which now at length are becoming in-

telligible to us in their vast import: words which IV.
distinctly lay down as elements of our spiritual consolation the dependence of Creation upon man both in his fall and in his restoration, the vital unity of the whole visible order which we are at present able to contemplate, the Divine law of progress by which all that is imperfect moves towards a second birth.

The expression of these truths is indeed, as I have said, unique, but the truths themselves fall in with the entire scope of Scripture; and the first lesson this afternoon (Is. lxv.) has reminded us that the renovation of the world forms as conspicuous a subject of the prophetic gospel as the renovation of society. It could not be otherwise, for the sympathy of Nature with man is written on the first page of the Bible and on the last. In
the spiritual history of Genesis the earth is said Gen. iii. 17.
to have been cursed for man's sake. In the
spiritual vision of the Apocalypse new heavens Apoc. xxi. 1.
and a new earth are prepared for redeemed humanity. Meanwhile the necessity of anxious toil, imposed upon us by the conditions of life in this season of our conflict, is designed by a Father's love for salutary discipline; and on the other hand we are encouraged to believe that *the earnest expectation of the Creation waiteth for the revealing of the sons of God,* waiteth, in due season,

IV. to reflect their glory even as they will reflect the
1 John iii. 2. glory of their Saviour at His Coming: waiteth, and yet not in mere idle and passive expectancy but to receive a blessing towards which it has striven through a discipline of fruitful suffering. *For the whole Creation groaneth and travaileth in pain together until now.*

The whole Creation groaneth and travaileth in pain together until now. Not at once and, in their fulness not at last, can we grasp the teaching of these wonderful words. But three points are sufficiently clear in them. They set before us the thoughts of a common life in Creation, of a life of pain, of a life of pain leading to a new birth.

1. There is a common life in Creation. Our own little life is for each one of us of such absorbing interest that we often use it to measure the idea of life itself. We can apply the standard successfully to those forms of life with which we are most familiar and which we can readily embrace in what appears to be their completeness. But, as we have already seen, the life of a nation, the life of humanity, the life of the Body of Christ, transcends its application. And now St Paul carries us beyond the ultimate societies of men. He leads us to see the functions of a common life in all Nature, in things irrational, and in things, as we speak, inanimate. He bids

us regard them as truly united in the circumstances of their present condition and of their future consummation. IV.

We observe so little and for so short a time: the play of forces around us is so complicated and so distracting; our point of sight is so completely immersed in the movement which we wish to calculate; that it is hopeless for us to seek for more than a dim sense of the immeasurable life which is thus suggested. But that sense alone, vague and fleeting as it may be, is inestimably precious. He who has gained it, he who has gained it and used it to give reality to his belief that it was the good pleasure of God *to sum up all things in Christ, the things in the heavens and the things upon the earth,* has gained that which is able to transfigure the aspect of the world. Eph. i. 10.

2. For this life of the Universe is for the present manifested to us in pain. *The whole Creation groaneth together.* Through all its parts there are to our sight marks of failure, of imperfection, of suffering; and these St Paul describes in the language of consciousness because that in which they are found is a living whole; and man cannot but express ideas of life in terms of his own life. But the language is no utterance, as has been most falsely said, of a

IV. 'pathetic fallacy.' It witnesses with commanding power, even in its sadness, to that kinsmanship of being which lies in a common divine origin. 'A world which God made dead?' Nay rather, death comes from sin, and we communicate the semblance of our deadness to our environment.

We communicate to our environment the semblance of our deadness, as we have communicated to it once for all the issues of our Fall. For no one, I suppose, can fail to have been struck with the inexpressibly sombre aspect which nature offers to our human sight. There is, as it must seem, a prodigal waste of life. A gust of wind sweeping along an avenue scatters over the ground seeds which might give birth to a forest, and not one of them is fruitful. There is a fierce struggle for existence, type against type, class against class, unit against unit; and the balance of parts in the organization of life is so delicate that a small change in one of them is sufficient to bring destruction to a whole race. There is the inherent incompleteness of life, which is such that no individual ever reaches the full measure of its characteristic energy or beauty. Everywhere we seem to read the same sad tale. Thousands are sacrificed to one, and that one fails.

3. It would be easy to pursue in detail the terrible indictment: easy to shew that, if, according

IV.

to the beautiful Greek fancy, the clay of which man was moulded was moistened not with water but with tears, every strain of natural music as it strikes upon our senses dies away into a dirge: easy to paint the ashy tint of death which follows the glow of burning purple on the mountain side when the sun has set: easy to round all in gloom, if we pause in our first experience. But we may not pause here. St Paul recognises the deep voice of grief in the Creation but he does not rest in it. *The whole Creation*, he says, *groaneth and travaileth together until now.* The sorrow is unto joy at last. Out of that which appears to us to be a confused struggle shall come a new and more perfect life. The pains which we witness are the very conditions of the birth of the new order. In this case also, as with man, the passage to life is through suffering. But we believe that not one agony is wasted, and in part we can justify our faith. The same facts which are full of sadness when referred to the individual are full of hope when referred to the whole. Constant rivalry under the actual conditions of earth—conditions which express the will of God—provides for a gradual elevation of type and in the long run that form survives which is best fitted for the work to be done. Under this aspect the largest

John xvi. 21.

IV. lessons of human life are reassuring. Races, kingdoms, societies, like individuals, pass away when they have fulfilled their part. They pass away, and yet they live on in the greater order which they have prepared; so that we already rejoice in the assurance that descendants better and nobler than ourselves will carry on and perfect that which we have rudely prepared. Nor do we stay here. We are constrained to think that this joy may find a place also in the larger realm of Nature. The prospect may be obscure in the present, from the imperfection of our powers, but at least what we do see justifies the picture which we draw. As far as we can look back the earth was slowly prepared through many changes, by fire and frost, by flood and earthquake, to be the scene of man's discipline; and since the time came for man to enter on his kingdom, his advance may fairly be taken as the measure of advance in all below him.

So far Nature alone guides us with lights fitful and scattered, yet kindled at a heavenly source. But now let the thought of the Incarnation come in, the thought that it was the Father's good pleasure from the first to rear through the ages a living shrine for His Word which became conscious in man, the thought that the eternal Son has taken to Himself the firstfruits of our terrestrial order in His Body through the grave to the throne of God: the thought that as *in Him were all things created* so *in Him all things consist*, and it is for us, I will dare to say, a new creation of the world. Every token of inner and manifold life in *all things in the heavens and upon the earth* assumes a fresh significance. The seed wasted, the feebler being swept away, the effort marred, have each their proper value and contribute to the fulness of the whole. In the tender love of that all-embracing Presence every unit stands out in clear distinctness from the innumerable host in which its sensible action is absorbed. The limits of the activity of finite being are not circumscribed by human experience. The world is not a great museum of specimens to be arranged with exhaustive knowledge, but a revelation of life, where knowledge is the herald of reverence and the minister of love. The progress of the past is the sign and not the measure of that which shall be when the glory of the sons of God shall be reflected by the scene of their finished labour; or rather when we with pure and opened eyes shall see the world as God made it. IV.

> "O world, as God has made it! All is beauty:
> And knowing this is love, and love is duty.
> What further may be sought for, or declared?"

IV. For even now, as I must think, faint, fragmentary traces of the splendid vision are being disclosed to us. There is (who does not know it?) much in the peculiar circumstances of our life and thought to disquiet and distress, but there is much also, much which is offered to us first by the Spirit of God, to compensate and calm our anxieties; much above all in those larger views of life which tend to make the fact of the Incarnation, I will venture to say, the most natural of all facts.

It may be that in our day of trial we shall fail to apprehend the new messages of widening wisdom: that we shall cling blindly to fixed traditional forms of opinion which do not correspond with the requirements of our spiritual position: that we shall seek to confine within artificial limits, through timorous distrust, that which is a power of infinite growth.

It may be: but innumerable voices fill us with a better hope. As yet indeed they are not blended into one prayer, one confession, one thanksgiving. But beneath their accidental and temporary discordances there is one ruling thought expressed in many ways, now with trembling pathos and now with unchastened boldness, the thought of one life, one Spirit, one Lord and Saviour, one God and Father of all. And the Gospel of Creation fulfilled in the Gospel of the Word made flesh is able to unite them. Not one secret won from Nature by unconscious interpreters of the Divine will, not one fact shewn to have been realised in history by the students of human progress, not one cry of penitence, or one aspiration of faith, which rises from the solitary soul, fails to find a place in the majestic range of that Gospel, fails, if we look aright, to shew it in more sovereign grace. IV.

The characteristic sign of the Messianic Presence on which the prophets dwelt, was 'the opening of the eyes of the blind': so may God in His mercy open *the eyes of our hearts* that we may behold the King Who comes to us in His beauty. More hangs upon our faith than mind can imagine or embrace. The work which through our ministry embodies the grace of Christ affects, by His will, not ourselves only, not our fellow-men only, but all things in heaven and on earth, all things which He has made as the image of His love. Even now, in the sight of our overmastering self-absorption, our faint endeavours, *the earnest expectation of the Creation waiteth for the revealing of the Sons of God.*

Is. xxxv. 5.

Eph. i. 18.

Is. xxxiii. 17.

V.

THE INCARNATION AND LIFE.

For of his fulness we all received, and grace for grace.

St John i. 16.

THE INCARNATION AND LIFE.

WE have hitherto considered the Incarnation V.
in relation to the widest thoughts of life and being, as the crown of the original purpose of Creation, as the fulfilment of the destiny of man in spite of sin, the fruit of self-assertion, as the revelation of the vital unity of Nature. The vision which is thus opened to devout contemplation is of such transcending splendour that there is a danger lest we should allow ourselves to be occupied with it, to be absorbed by it, to be lost in it, as it were, in a kind of indolent optimism. We are tempted to say when we gain a faint impression of the magnificent range of the divine order, and of the unexpected ways in which the divine counsel is accomplished, 'It is enough: the will of God will be fulfilled. What can we do?'

True, most true. The will of God will be fulfilled. Its execution does not depend upon our

v. endeavour. But O the difference for each one of us, if we behold it, if we enter into it, if, in our poor measure, we make it our own, if we offer ourselves without reserve for its service. And it is for this reason, we must believe, we are allowed to discern a little of its course. For the noblest truths are not given us for an intellectual luxury still less for a moral opiate or a spiritual charm. They are for the inspiration of our whole being, for the hallowing and for the bracing of every power outward and inward with which we are endowed, for use in the busy fields of common duty.

Truth, in a word, cannot remain as a possession of one part of our nature. If the deed is precious for the sake of the thought of which it is the fruit, the thought must vindicate its power by the corresponding deed. Man, as he is, is not fully revealed till thought is embodied in deed. And when Descartes had said 'I think, therefore I am,' I cannot but rejoice that our own Whichcote silently corrected the famous sentence by the more memorable phrase 'I act, therefore I am.'

And so the greatest of all truths, the truth of the Incarnation, reaches to the innermost recesses of the single life, that it may rouse and guide and sustain him who has welcomed it. It is, as we have seen, a revelation of love, of sin, of attainment, of sympathy: and it is all this to the individual soul. It is a revelation of humility, of suffering, of faith, issuing in exceeding glory, and it is all this to the solitary believer, self-surrendered, cast down, straining in unwearied effort towards the end which will not disappoint. V.

St John sets this reflection before us in the Introduction to his Gospel with sublime simplicity. We can hardly miss it if we follow only his main statements, and pass over the parenthetic illustrations with which he explains and enforces them:

In the beginning, we read, *was the Word and the Word was with God and the Word was God.* John i. 1, 14, 16.

And the Word became flesh and dwelt among us full of grace and truth.

Because out of His fulness all we received and grace for grace.

The Evangelist passes, we see, without one break from the contemplation of the eternal Majesty of God to the common experience of his fellow Christians. They all had, he assumes, direct personal knowledge of the power of Christ answering to His Nature no less than Apostles who had beheld His glory. The Word, as he teaches, finds a place naturally on the throne of the Father and in the heart of man.

Out of His fulness all we received and grace for John i. 16.

V. *grace.* The words express two main thoughts. The absolute perfection of all divine power and grace as it can be expressed through humanity is in Christ; in that fact lies the assurance of faith. And again the believer draws from Christ, as from an inexhaustible source, so much vital force as former effort has made him able to use: in that fact lies the law of the activity of faith. All that any man ever can be is already realised in the Son of man: each man as he puts to use one gift grows capable of receiving a greater.

These thoughts, full of encouragement and of warning, find a typical foreshadowing in a beautiful Jewish legend. It is said that when the Lord spoke from Sinai the voice was heard by the people as they turned this way and that, from North and South from East and West, from earth and heaven. The voice went forth throughout the world and each nation heard it in their own tongue. But they who heard heard it according to their capacity; old men and youths and boys and sucklings and women; and the voice was to each one as each one had power to receive it.

So men pictured to themselves the giving of the Law; and when the Word was manifested that which they had thus fancied became reality. From all sides, in every heart of man, His Message which is Himself found, as it still finds, expression and welcome according to the power of love. V.

Out of His fulness all we received. The perfect assurance of faith rests, I say, in this conviction. In Christ the Word Incarnate, the divine, the eternal, shines through the forms of earth unclouded and undimmed. If there were found in Him one trait which belonged to some transitory phase of human growth, to a sect, a class, a nation, an age, if there were wanting in Him one characteristic which belongs to the essence of humanity; one virtue which is the peculiar glory of man or woman; we might then *look for another* to fulfil the higher type which we Matt. xi. 3.
should be able to imagine. But as it is, there is nothing which we can remove from His portraiture, nothing which we can add to it, without marring the ideal in which each soul can find the satisfaction of every desire that it would lay open in the light of heaven. We believe—it is a belief to ponder—that our highest conceivable has been realised by *the Word become flesh* under the conditions of earth. We believe not that one man by the cultivation of natural powers has striven upwards to fellowship with God, but that the Son of God has taken humanity to Himself and gained that for the race which each member can find for himself in Him. We

v. believe that that Life of Jesus of Nazareth matured in silent obscurity and closed in open shame, that life gladdened only by the joys which are open to the least of the children of men, the glories of the sky and field, and the response of loyal hearts, is the life in which our destiny has been reached once for all. We believe this, and in our impatient strugglings, in our grasping at shadows, in our sad murmurings, the belief seems to be on the point of vanishing; but if it vanishes for a time it is only to reappear in the darkness, like stars in the night to witness of other worlds.

The belief—the belief in the divine fulness of Christ—is indeed one which it is not easy to keep in the freshness of its energy. The ideal which it proposes is ever escaping from us under the pressure of sordid cares and fears. But we gain no relief from labour by lowering our standard. We do not rid ourselves of enigmas by abridging our hopes. We cast away the Faith; and what then? The sufferings of earth remain, but they are emptied of their redemptive potency. The questionings of practical knowledge remain, but no response comes with a Gospel of grace and truth. The mysteries of the finite remain, but they are not lightened by the assurance that the human conceptions by which we live as to things of sense may be trusted no less as to things unseen. V.

Not one difficulty, one pain, one contradiction of life is removed by the spirit of denial. Only the treasury of heaven is closed at its bidding; and we are charged to stand resigned with our faces turned towards an impenetrable gloom, through which the Christian sees a pathway of light, even the glorified humanity of Christ, leading to the throne of God. Hebr. x. 19 f.

Out of His fulness we all received: 'out of His fulness:' not from ourselves though in ourselves is the spring of strength. For Christ's gift, as it has free course, must stir us with the impulse of a great devotion. Conscious of our own sins and of our own forgiveness we shall have learnt to see the world in a new light. Touched by the love of Christ we shall feel love. Compassion will gain for us again its true meaning. We shall minister to the weak and the erring not in condescending pity but as enabled to share evils which are indeed our own. The power of our action, as we look to the Son of God Incarnate, will be not fear or sorrow, not even the sense of right, but reverence for the divine in man.

Out of His fulness we all received and grace for grace. 'Grace for grace:' that is the inexorable law of the Spirit, the law of the activity of faith.

v. The higher, nobler, fuller, comes to men only as the fruit of the lower and the less.

'Light after light well-used they shall attain.'

And in this condition lies for us the promise of joy growing with growing life. As each successive lesson of the Incarnation is learnt, the spirit yet
John xvi. 14. again takes of that which is Christ's, and shews it to the believer. There can be no repetition and no rest in His teaching. At the same time we need to be reminded continually of the learner's obligation and of the blessing which the obligation carries. For of all the perils of advancing age none, as I have said before, is greater than that of losing the faculty of wonder. We become familiar with the sequence of phenomena and we think that we understand them. They move us no longer with the surprise of freshness. But for the thoughtful the increase of such knowledge as we can gain adds to the mysteries of life. That which is commonest is indeed the most real cause for wonder. In this sense the materials of wonder are continually gathered about us. And when the Lord said to the Jews who were perplexed by His works and
John v. 20. His claims *greater works than these will* [the Father] *shew* [the Son], *that ye may marvel,* He declared the manner of His revelation. From age

to age He offers to us *grace for grace.* He dis- v.
closes in the ordinary conditions of life to those who *have their senses exercised by use* 'greater works' than their fathers saw, more far-reaching connexions, subtler harmonies, deeper beauties of life, 'that they may marvel' not in idle astonishment or in vacant curiosity, but as looking beyond the signs to the spiritual forces which they suggest. Hebr. v. 14.

Yes: that is one of the main lessons of the Incarnation. It is ever leading us through the seen to the unseen, offering in this way *grace for grace;* and so it is that Christianity in consideration of our natures is essentially Sacramental. So it is that God is pleased to take the outward as the channel of His working: that he uses the commonest things for the highest ends: that He binds together the material and the spiritual, in a union of life: even in order that we may extend the revelation to all parts of the order in which we are placed, that we may feel that we are at every point in contact with unseen powers, that reverence may rest wherever knowledge enters.

At the same time this revelation of the spiritual grandeur of all life enhances the importance of the single life. Each single life is seen in the Incarnation to be in the divine plan an element in the Body of Christ; and we come

V. to understand, when we meditate on the dependences of things, how in the vast chorus of Creation one voice of 'little human praise' is missed.

And not only does each life gain this solemn significance from its relation to the vaster life in which it is included, but each least part of the individual life assumes a proportionate value. Nothing can be of the man only: nothing can be of the body only. The deed of the member, of the member of the society, of the member of the family, reaches as far as the life reaches, even if we have at present no powers to measure its effects.

This conviction of the illimitable consequences of action would be of overwhelming awfulness if we were not able to lift our eyes when the burden is heaviest to the Son of man; if we were not able to bring to Him the stained and fragmentary offering of ourselves and to find in Him that which is needed to cleanse and to complete it. We look back indeed for a moment upon the long line of witnesses whose works, on which we have entered, attest the efficacy of His unfailing Presence, but then we *look away* from all else (ἀφορῶντες) *to* Heb. xii. 2.
Jesus the leader and perfecter of faith, Who in His humanity met every temptation which can assail us and crowned with sovereign victory the force which He offers for our support.

By such experience, such efforts, such reflections we learn in the stress of life, *receiving grace for grace,* that the Incarnation is more than an event: that it is a Truth. We learn that it is a fact not in the sense that it is past but that it is eternal. We learn that the fulfilment of the Incarnation in time is the revelation of that which is beyond time; the absolute, may we not say the necessary, seal to us men of the certainty of the ideas which we are led to fashion under human conditions of the righteousness and love of God, of the grandeur of the heritage for which we were born, of the melancholy sentence of failure which is written against us, of the hope which we cannot forego that we shall yet see God, see God and live. V.

We meditate on these conclusions; and while we do so we recognise that the Incarnation reconciles the last terms of that contradiction in life to what our greatest poets and some of the most influential teachers of the time bear witness. For in our noblest literature we find on the one side a stern and pitiless description of dominant evil and sorrow, of duty to be sadly if resolutely followed, of multitudes who can only be dealt with by some crushing force: and on the other side we hear a confident appeal to the instinct of beauty and goodness, to the triumphs of natural heroism,

V. to the soul of man which struggles through freedom to the light. We are met, that is, on the one side by the thought of law without the reality of redemption: and on the other side by the thought of love without the reality of the fall.

There is the contradiction from which Nature opens no escape; but in the Incarnation, as a fact, nay as *the* fact of human life, the fall and the redemption both find complete expression. In the Incarnation law and love are seen in their final harmony.

Brethren, we have touched upon great mysteries, mysteries to be 'kept and pondered in our hearts.' In dealing with them words and thoughts are alike inadequate. So far as these become definite they tend to limit that which is infinite. But their imperfection is not unavailing if it encourages us to strive by the help of the Holy Spirit—and it is a hard task—to know that the revelation of God given to us in the Incarnation is given by a living fact, not in a speculation or in a dogma. Forms of thought change, but this Fact vivifies and transcends all.

As a Fact the Incarnation presents intelligibly before our eyes an aim towards which we can bend every energy of our nature.

As a Fact it supplies a motive which stirs V.
us to devout exertion with an energy proportioned to the faith with which we apprehend its essence.

As a Fact it is of infinite meaning and able to minister all that is needed for the hallowing of toil and study.

As a Fact it is of infinite power, and sufficient to assure help to the weakest servant of God.

As a Fact it shews us how that unity to which physics and history point is not to be found only in a dispersive connexion of multitudinous parts, but is summed up finally in One Who is God.

As a Fact it supplies a solid foundation for the loftiest aspirations which man ever fashioned for himself in the personal consciousness of unsatisfied longings.

As a Fact, an eternal Fact, realised in time, may we receive it, hold it, reflect upon it. So shall we know day by day a little more what it involves, what it promises, what it enforces, what it inspires. So shall we draw strength and wisdom from the very speculations which at first sight appear to be fraught with danger. So shall we do the part to which we are called in the building up of the Church. So shall we offer our little lives, marred and broken as they are, to Him Who is able to bring them into fellowship with Him-

V. self. Let us hear once again the Gospel on which we have been allowed to meditate. *The Word became flesh and dwelt among us...full of grace and truth...because out of His fulness we all received and grace for grace.*

APPENDIX.

THE VISION OF GOD THE CALL OF THE PROPHET.

Holy, holy, holy, is the Lord of hosts: the whole earth is full of His glory.

Is. vi. 3.

TWO years ago it was my duty to speak here as on this day; and now, when I am unexpectedly called to fulfil the same office, my thoughts necessarily go back to the words of the angelic hymn on which I dwelt then. In some form or other the feelings which they express must fill all our hearts. As often as the Festival of the Holy Trinity—the Festival of Revelation—comes round, we are encouraged to lift up our eyes to the manifestation of the divine glory. And through this reverent effort we learn with growing assurance that the contemplation of the majesty of God is the source of the largest hope for all His creatures. We come to understand how for beings pure and holy that vision is the call to unfaltering adoration and limitless faith; how for men "of unclean lips," sin-stained and labouring in a sin-stained world, it is the call, the reassuring call, to the prophet's work.

This, then, is the thought which I wish to

APPENDIX. welcome for myself from the services of the day. This is the thought which I wish to commend to those who hear me: that the vision of God is the call of the prophet; that the vision of God given to us to-day in the Triune Name is our call, our message, our chastening.

1. The vision of God is, I say, the call of the prophet. Nowhere is the thought presented to us in the Bible with more moving force than in
Is. vi. 1-10. the record of Isaiah's mission which we heard again this morning. The very mark of time by which the history is introduced has a pathetic significance. It places together in sharp contrast the hasty presumption of man and the unchanging love of God. The prophet was called in the year
2 Chron. xxvi. 16 ff. that King Uzziah died. The king died an outcast and a leper because he had ventured to take to himself the function of a priest in the house of God; and in close connexion with that tragic catastrophe an access to God, far closer than that which the successful monarch had prematurely claimed, was foreshewn to the prophet in a heavenly figure. Isaiah, a layman, as you remember, was, it appears, in the temple court, and he saw in a trance the way into the holiest place laid open. The veils were removed from sanctuary and shrine, and he beheld more than met the
Lev. xvi. eyes of the high priest, the one representative of the people, on the one day on which he was

admitted year by year to the dark chamber which shrouded the divine presence. He beheld not the glory resting upon the symbolic ark, but the Lord sitting upon the throne high and lifted up; not the carved figures of angels, but the seraphim standing with outstretched wings, ready for swift service; not the vapour of earthly incense, but the cloud of smoke which witnessed to the Majesty which it hid. This opening of "the eyes of his heart" was God's gift, God's call to him. Other worshippers about the young prophet saw, as we must suppose, nothing but "the light of common day," the ordinary sights of the habitual service, the great sea of brass, and the altar of burnt-offering, and the stately portal of the holy place, and Priests and Levites busy with their familiar work. But for an eternal moment Isaiah's senses were unsealed. He saw that which is and not that which appears. For him the symbol of God dwelling in light unapproachable, was transformed into a personal presence; for him the chequered scene of human labour and worship was filled with the train of God; for him the marvels of human skill were instinct with the life of God. The spot which God had chosen was disclosed to his gaze as the centre of the divine revelation; but at the same time he was taught to acknowledge that the Divine Presence is not limited by any bounds or excluded by any blindness, when

APPENDIX. he heard from the lips of angels that the fulness
Is. vi. 3. of the whole earth is His glory.

Now when we recall what Judaism was at the time, local, rigid, exclusive, we can at once understand that such a vision, such a revelation taken into the soul, was for Isaiah an illumination of the world. He could at last see all creation in its true nature through the light of God. So to have looked upon it was to have gained that which the seer, cleansed by the sacred fire, was constrained to declare. Humbled, and purified in his humiliation, he could have but one answer when the voice of the Lord required a messenger, "Here am I: send me."

And as it was then it is now. If that response of Isaiah seems to us, as it must do, to be natural or even necessary when we realise his position, let us not shrink from the confession that Isaiah's vision, Isaiah's call, are for us also, and that they await from us a like response. When the prophet Isaiah looked upon that
John xii. 41. august sight he saw, as St John tells us, Christ's glory; he saw in figures and far off that which we have been allowed to contemplate more nearly and with the power of closer apprehension. He saw in transitory shadows that which we have received in a historic Presence. By the Incarnation God has entered, and empowered us to feel that He has entered, into fellowship with humanity

and men. As often as that truth rises before our eyes, all heaven is indeed rent open, and all earth is displayed as God made it. For us, then, the vision and the call of Isaiah find a fuller form, a more sovereign voice in the Gospel than the Jewish prophet could know. And I will dare to believe that there is not one among us who has not been quickened to see here, in this home of generous enthusiasm, glimpses of the prophet's vision, when he has pondered in some quiet space of thought the need of the prophet's work in England or in India; to see disclosed before him the inner sanctuary of Truth and Love; to see on the Father's throne, high and lifted up, the Lord who had lived and died and risen again for him; to see the folds of His imperial vesture spread over the whole world, which is His dwelling-place; to see innumerable hosts of ministering spirits fulfilling His word in the wide realm of nature; to see the signs of His Presence, half-splendour and half-cloud, made known through all the works of men; to see messengers sent "with live coals from off the altar" to purify and to kindle those who shall bear the Gospel to the nations.

Brethren, if, as I believe, you have seen this, dimly, it may be, and but for a brief moment, and you above all before whom the work of life is opening with the fresh fulness of promise in the purpose of God's grace, be sure that there is

APPENDIX. nothing in life more real than such a vision. It is the pure light of heaven so broken by the shadows of earth that we can bear it. Do not then turn from it, or dismiss it as a dream. Meet it with the response of glad devotion. It is easy, alas, to question the authority of the greatest thoughts which God sends to us. It is easy to darken them and to lose them. But it is not easy to live on to the end without them. There is, happily, a noble discontent which disturbs all self-centred pleasure. And, on the other hand, you must have been allowed to feel that you are stirred with the truest joy, and braced to labour best at your little tasks, while you welcome and keep before you the loftiest ideal of the method and the aim of work and being which God has made known to you. That is, indeed, His revelation, the vision of Himself. So He declares what He would have you to do, what He will enable you to do. So He calls you to be prophets.

Yes; for us the vision of God, the vision of this day is a prophet's call. And let us gratefully recognise the divine order in which it is presented to us. The Festival of Revelation follows the Festival of the Spirit. The Festival of the Spirit closes the cycle of the historic festivals of the Church. And now all the facts of the historic Gospel are crowned by the thought of God in Himself; and that thought, summed up in the

Triune Name into which we were baptised, is APPENDIX.
offered to us afresh to-day for calm study. We
are called upon to use the "power from on high Luke xxiv. 49.
with which we have been clothed," to regard yet
once again with questioning devotion the secret
of the eternal life which has been made known to
us for the use of earth in the Person of Christ.

And what, therefore, we ask, does *the mystery,* the revelation *of God, even Christ,* mean for Col. ii. 2.
us, the mystery of which we are ministers and
prophets, the mystery which brings the eternal
within the forms of time, the mystery which shews
to us absolute love made visible in the Incarnate
Word? It means—it must mean if only we
think patiently and calmly—that the outward,
the transitory, is a veil woven by the necessities
of our weakness which half hides and half reveals
the realities with which it corresponds; it means
that the changing forms in which spiritual aspirations are clothed from generation to generation
and from life to life, are illuminated, quickened,
harmonised in one supreme fact; it means that
beyond the temples in which it is our blessing to
worship and beyond the phrases which it is our
joy to affirm, there is an infinite glory which can
have no local circumscription, and an infinite
Truth which cannot be grasped by any human
thought; it means that man, bruised and burdened by sorrows and sins, was made for God, and

APPENDIX. that through His holy love he shall not fail of his destiny; it means that all creation is an expression of God's thought of wisdom brought within the reach of human intelligence; it means that God's Spirit sent in His Son's name will interpret little by little, as we can read the lesson, all things as contributory to His praise; it means that we also, compassed with infirmities and burdened with sins, may take up the song of the redeemed creation, the song of the unfallen angels, and say, "Holy, holy, holy, is the Lord of hosts: the fulness of the earth is His glory." It means this, and more than this, more than mind can shape and tongue can utter, and as the light streams in upon us we cannot refuse to acknowledge the obligation by which we are bound to make known that which is made plain by its brightness; to interpret to others according to the teaching of our own experience the truth which has been disclosed to our souls.

John xiv. 26.

2. For even as the vision of God is the call of the prophet, so it is this vision which the prophet has to proclaim and to interpret to his fellow-men, not as an intellectual theory, but as an inspiration of life. The prophet's teaching must be the translation of his experience. He bears witness of that which he has seen. His words are not an echo but a living testimony. The heart alone can speak to the heart. But he

who has beheld the least fragment of the divine glory, he who has spelt out in letters of light on the face of the world one syllable of the Triune Name, will have a confidence and a power which nothing else can bring. Only let him trust what he has seen, and it will become to him a guiding-star till he rests in the unveiled Presence of Christ.

And so let us all thank God, on this Festival of Revelation, that He has called us in the fulfilment of our prophet's office to unfold a growing message and not to rehearse a stereotyped tradition. The Gospel of Christ Incarnate, the Gospel of the Holy Trinity in the terms of human life, which we have to announce, covers every imaginable fact of life to the end of time, and is new now as it has been new in all the past, as it will be new, new in its power and new in its meaning, while the world lasts. It was new when St John at Ephesus was enabled to express its fundamental truth in the doctrine of the Word; new when Athanasius at Nicæa affirmed through it the living unity of the Godhead without derogating from the Lord's Deity; new when Anselm at Bec sought in it, however partially and inadequately, a solution of the problem of eternal justice; new when Luther at Wittenberg found in it the ground of personal communion with God; new in our own generation, new with an untold message,

APPENDIX. when we are bidden to acknowledge in it the pledge of that ultimate fellowship of created things which the latest researches in nature and in history offer for consecration.

For this supreme unity, which is neither monotonous nor barren, and nothing less than this, answers, as I have already indicated, to that vision of God in Christ, "the true God," "the God of hope," which is presented to this age. And we therefore as we behold the Divine Image under the light of our own day must labour to bring to our view of "the world"—the order for a time separated from God—that thought of God which makes it again a fit object of our love as it is the object of the love of God; to bring to our view of society that conviction of dependence and connexion which is at once a safeguard and a motive force: to bring to our view of the present that sense of eternity which transfigures our estimate of great and small, of success and failure.

John xvii. 3. Rom. xv. 13.

John iii. 16.

The transformation of life requires no more: it is possible with no less. And to us as Christians the charge is given to bear this prophetic message to men.

True it is that such a vision of God—Creator, Redeemer, Sanctifier—entering into fellowship with the beings whom He has made, "reconciling all things unto Himself, having made peace through the blood of the Cross," shews life to us, as

Col. i. 20.

Isaiah saw it, in a most solemn aspect: that it must fill us, as it filled Isaiah, with the sense of our immeasurable unworthiness in the face of Christ's majesty and Christ's love: that it must touch us also with something of a cleansing power. And because it is so we can take heart again. APPENDIX.

For such emotion, such purification of soul, is the beginning of abiding strength, "He that wonders shall reign;" "He that is near me is near fire," are among the few traditional sayings attributed to the Lord which seem to be stamped as divine. Awe, awe the lowliest and the most self-suppressing, is a sign not of littleness, but of nobility. Our power of reverence is a measure of our power of rising. As we bow in intelligent worship before the face of our King, His Spirit—a Spirit of fire—enters into us. We feel that we are made partakers of the Divine nature because we can acknowledge with a true faith its spiritual glories, and lay ourselves

> Passive and still before the awful Throne . . .
> Consumed, yet quickened, by the glance of God.

3. So we come to the last consideration which I desire to suggest. The vision of God is, as we have seen, the call of the prophet, and the message of the prophet. It is also the chastening of the prophet.

And in the fulfilment of our prophetic work

APPENDIX. we need, I think, more than we know the abasing and elevating influences which the vision of Isaiah and the thoughts of to-day are fitted to create or deepen. In the stress of restless occupation we are tempted to leave too much out of sight the inevitable mysteries of life. We deal lightly with the greatest questions. We are peremptory in defining details of dogma beyond the teaching of Scripture. We are familiar beyond apostolic precedent in our approaches to God. We fashion heavenly things after the fashion of earth. We are like Mary Magdalene, who in her mistaken love would have kept her
John xx. 17. Lord as she had first known Him, when as yet the Ascension had not revealed the nature of an eternal fellowship, and made such fellowship possible; and once more Christ, as we recognise Him at first under the conditions of earth, seems to be saying to us, "'Cling not to me,' not with the hand but with the soul must you hold Me if you would enjoy My abiding presence."

In all these respects then, for our strengthening and for our purifying, we must seek for ourselves and strive to spread about us the sense of the awfulness of being, as those who have seen
Apoc. iv. 2 f. God at Bethlehem, Calvary, Olivet, and on the throne encircled by a rainbow as an emerald: the sense, vague and imperfect at the best, of the illimitable range of the courses and issues of

action; the sense of the untold vastness of that life which we are bold to measure by our feeble powers; the sense of the Majesty of Him before Whom the angels veil their faces. If we are cast down by the meannesses, the sorrows, the sins of the world, it is because we dwell on some little part of which we see little; but let the thought of God in Christ come in, and we can rest in that holy splendour. At the same time let us not dare to confine at our will the action of the light. It is our own irreparable loss if in our conceptions of doctrine we gain clearness of definition by following out the human conditions of apprehending the divine, and forget that every outline is the expression in terms of a lower order of that which is many sided; if in our methods of devotion we single out the human nature of the Lord, or rather the manifestation of His unascended manhood, as the object of our thoughts, and forget that He leads us to the Father; if we rest in things visible and do not rather strive to read ever more clearly the spiritual lessons to which they point; if we concentrate our worship in isolated rites and fail to bear to the world of daily thought and action the teaching and the promises of Sacraments.

Brethren, the thoughts on which we have touched open unfathomable depths of duty. But it is good for us to reflect on the greatness of God

APPENDIX. which is as immeasurable as His love. And may He in His great mercy cleanse our dull eyes, and check our hasty tongues, and calm our impetuous reasonings; and so in the solemn calm the vision of Him—Father, Son, and Holy Ghost—will take shape slowly before us. So we shall still recognise in it our call, our message, our spirit, as prophets touched by His fire. We shall say with the lowliest confession of our unworthiness, "our eyes have seen the King, the Lord of Hosts." We shall reply with the most absolute self-surrender to the voice which asks in our hearts for messengers to make truth known, each according to our ability: "Here am I: send me." And in the lifelong fulfilment of our work, undismayed by the darkness which we cannot penetrate, undeterred by the weakness which we cannot overcome, we shall repeat the song of heaven, which the Incarnation has fitted for the lips of men, "Holy, holy, holy, is the Lord of hosts, the fulness of the earth is His glory."

ST MARY'S, CAMBRIDGE.
Trinity Sunday, 1885.